OUR HIDDEN WORLD

ON THE ORIGINS OF FORM

OLAM
BOOK ONE

IAN F TERRY

ON MAPS, MEANING, AND METAPHYSICS

This isn't a book about religion. It's about the metaphysical questions that religion was created to explore, and now science is trying to answer with models and data.

Every metaphysical system is a map. A way our brain organizes, makes sense of, and navigates the infinite world inside and around us. Language is a prime example: a deeply shared, yet wildly imprecise system that enables us to recognize ideas, emotions, or physical objects by naming them. "Book," for instance, is a four-letter symbol we've collectively agreed means "a bundle of pages filled with words." But it's not the thing itself, but rather a shortcut, or heuristic. A key on the map. Just a tool.

This book explores the tools that shape our internal maps, are how they are drawn, redrawn, confused, and clarified through instinct, language, culture, belief, and environment.

When we mistake the map for the real territory, a fracture opens in our capacity to navigate; we begin to move through symbols rather than the world, and it is this severance that causes our suffering.

I was raised deeply Christian. I do not believe in God as a literal being, but naturally carry the stories that were part of my beginning.

I never really believed in God, but my first memory of exploring the idea was when I was ten. My best friend Brandon fell into a coma from a brain tumor. I was in Germany at the time. I remember waking suddenly in the night and looking at the clock. It read 00:00, and something about that moment unnerved me: zero hour. I got up and went downstairs. My parents were with the friends we were staying with; their eyes were red. They had learned Brandon had fallen unconscious; he would never wake up.

I recall standing in the shower and praying with all my might, asking God to take me instead. I said he could have my life if Brandon could keep his. Of course, nothing happened.

That silence was confirmation for me; it marked the beginning of the quest to separate our religious beliefs from our empirical ones. It began a long journey from Christianity to Judaism, to Buddhism, and ultimately to the metaphysical framework that underpins this book. While I do not believe in a god, I believe in 'incarnation' as a metaphor beyond the miracle; the divine becoming human to understand what it means to fear, long, and suffer. This story, and all the others, still matter.

It's echoed in Buddhist thought, Hindu avatars, and indigenous cosmologies where the sacred appears as animals, rivers, wind, and volcanoes.

The message is this: life itself is the medium of understanding. We come to *know* through living, through *incarnating* as different selves, ideas, roles, and organisms. And from that knowing, we evolve.

This book explores this idea as an experiment along a path without a specific destination. We'll be talking about instinct, environment, language, consciousness, and belief. I have no intention of having a final say on any topic, but I wish to navigate within them, to iterate on the maps we've inherited and explore how we might redraw them.

It's okay to be wrong. I am wrong quite often. Being 'wrong' is one of the fastest ways to get closer to something true. Western thought usually obsesses over what something is. But we must also train ourselves to learn from what something is not, and all the degrees in between. By doing so, we not only pursue accuracy but also cultivate humility and wisdom.

So let's begin, not with certainty but with attention, and see where the spiral leads.

ON THE ORIGINS
OF FORM

Welcome to *Our Hidden World* the first book in the *Olam series*, books about the hidden structures that shape our world.

At first glance, humans seem full of contradictions. We are animals with language. We build cities and satellites, yet we still act from fear and desires we cannot fully control. Many of our societies value individual freedom, yet they are always enmeshed in systems, cultures, and inherited beliefs. We strive for 'truth' as a concept, while clinging to maps drawn long before we could name them.

This book is an invitation to gently sift through these inherited maps with enough clarity to choose what we will carry forward.

Our Hidden World explores the layered structure of experience: how our environment shapes our instincts, how those instincts scaffold consciousness, and how consciousness loops back to redesign the environment.

This spiral exists like this:

Inorganic→ Biological → Cultural → Intellectual

Or we could say:

Environment —> Instinct —> Consciousness

These are the lived architecture of human evolution, and we'll get into how I developed them. But its important to note that they are simply two ways of looking at the same spiral.

The environmental layer is simply the inorganic world, and the biological components of things that are not within us. The Instinct layer is simply the biology within us, as well as the subconscious cultural influences. The consciousness layer is simply the cultural influences that are conscious, mixed with our intellectual patterns. We decide where we want to draw the lines on the maps we make, so choose whichever you like (or make your own!).

While these spirals repeat, they are not closed. With each loop, new forms emerge. The systems we build, from rituals to algorithms, carry the imprint of our inner lives and those of the ones who came before us. Those systems then shape how we think, relate to, and embody.

Living consciously within this spiral is about practicing a new design, not just of tools, but of meaning.

HOW THIS BOOK IS STRUCTURED

The following chapters trace this spiral as a lived pattern. Each chapter builds on the one before it, revealing how layers of reality interact and how meaning arises through relationships.

- **Chapter 1** begins in the body, tracing our evolutionary roots and the instincts that still govern us.

- **Chapter 2** turns inward, exploring how we construct internal maps using language, belief, and story to make sense of our experiences.
- **Chapter 3** zooms out to examine the environments we inherit and design: ecosystems, cities, and digital worlds.
- **Chapter 4** introduces *Olamic Design,* a concept I call metaphysical engineering, a way of designing systems with awareness of the deeper structures they shape.
- **Chapter 5** names the terms we need to discuss these systems with care, precision, and coherence, and invites the reader to practice.
- **Chapter 6** returns to that practice: how to live the spiral; to see, name, and design with intention.

If you've ever felt torn between your instincts and ideals, or sensed that modern life is out of step with something more profound and older, this book is for you. It is not an answer. It offers a mirror, a compass, and a way of tracing meaning back to its roots.

Let's begin by returning to something ancient: the animal we still are.

CHAPTER I

THE ANIMAL WE STILL ARE

THE FIRST LAYER

In western wind her dwelling stands,
grain still rough in unlearned hands.
She shaped ash till ash drew blood,
and silence taught what it could.

Humans have long separated ourselves from the animals and beings around us. Even in the word *mankind*, we see this tendency to define ourselves not simply as part of nature, but as a distinct kind within it. Our scientific name reinforces this idea: *Homo sapiens sapiens*. The genus is *Homo*, meaning "human," and the species name *sapiens* means "wise." But we are not just *Homo sapiens*. We are *Homo sapiens sapiens*, literally, "wise wise human."

The repetition isn't an error. It's a classification choice, made to distinguish modern humans from earlier ancestors like *Homo sapiens idaltu*. But its effect is telling. We doubled the word for wisdom to underscore our separation, not just from other animals, but from previous versions of ourselves. The name reads like a metaphysical claim: not only are we the ones who know, we are the ones who know we know.

That desire to set ourselves apart, to be a category unto ourselves, may seem harmless. But it creates a dangerous gap in understanding our place in the world. It turns us inward and upward, rather than outward and embedded. It fractures the continuity of life into false divisions: us and them, human and animal, mind and matter.

This is not just a philosophical error. It is what I call a spiral rupture. When we design systems on top of that split and build ethics, technologies, or institutions that forget we are animals first, we sever the foundation on which everything else rests.

I'll return to the more profound consequences of that fracture later. But for now, we begin where the split began: with our instincts. Before we defined ourselves as different, we evolved as animals. And by tracing those instincts, understanding how they work, where they originated, and how they shape perception, we can begin to ask different questions. Not

"What makes us special?" but "What made us *believe* we were?"

The human mind's organic structures and its creation's evolutionary nature have imposed very stringent, yet knowable, constraints on the instinctual mechanisms within our brains. These instincts are the first map layers we inherit, etched not in symbols but in neural reflexes. Our minds are built like evolutionary building blocks; we have structures similar to those of the first vertebrates, which control our involuntary actions, such as breathing, blinking, and beating our hearts. This part of our brain also controls our muscle movements; we don't have to think the thought "move your arm." It's a subconscious communication deeply ingrained in the system since the first animals moved.

This brain structure operates even beneath what most of us consider our "subconscious," as does most of our mental processing. We don't consciously think in our toes or stomachs, and we do not notice how much of the world our brain chooses to ignore without input. The center of our "central nervous system" is not the majority of it; it's simply where our concept of "I" has become focused.

This centralization of identity into the cognitive organ has been occurring throughout the evolution of the animal kingdom for a long time. But the whole body still thinks. Ancient fish and other sea creatures developed "fight or flight" instincts that underpin the "you or them" thought process still used by almost every animal on this planet as the fundamental structure of most of their daily behavior. Even humans, who claim to be incredibly conscious beings, hardly perceive the nature of this nearly instantaneous process that governs how we encounter situations throughout our day.

Whether we feel fear or comfort, joy or aggression, isn't something we choose. It's triggered by a system far older than thought. It is an evolutionary mechanism that has been passed down for millions of years. This mechanism acts independently; it doesn't require language or seek permission. It simply responds.

Most of the time, it doesn't even speak to our conscious minds. It only surfaces when the stress is high enough to override whatever else we're doing. And by the time we notice, it's already acted.

Everything evolved after our earliest instincts were built upon that system. Mammals developed systems for evaluating status, territory, and social belonging. These systems don't override the fight-or-flight response; they filter it. Before acting, the brain now checks: How important is this? Who outranks whom? What happens if I lose?

Most of our daily interactions are shaped by this tension. A core impulse pushing us forward, and a hierarchy calculator holding it back.

This isn't abstract; it's structure. When we design corporate, social, and technological systems that ignore this layered reality, we create incoherence at the second layer of the spiral, the biological(instinct) layer.

STATUS AND SIMULATION

You can see this in any crowd: body language, eye contact, and posture. There is a constant negotiation between fear, desire, and perceived rank. A bar fight is one visible extreme. The aggressor's body runs a fight script, but it's mixed with a judgment: this person is weak enough that I can win. Whether they're right or wrong is almost irrelevant in the moment. Their behavior emerges from a rapid, layered, mostly unconscious process. Those around them react similarly, adjusting based on the aggressor's posture, tone, and status cues. Within seconds, everyone's subconscious has run a full social simulation.

But this doesn't only happen in bars. Most modern humans live in a kind of constant pre-fight state; not because we're experiencing violence constantly, but because the pace and pressures of society prime us to be ready to react. We're socially anxious, overstimulated, and often unsure of our place. When people feel threatened but also powerless, aggression turns inward or sideways. That's passive-aggression, road rage, and doomscrolling with envy: hours spent scrolling through headlines and curated lives, watching others succeed while feeling stuck.

This isn't a failure of character but a mismatch of layers. Our environment is abstract, fast, and symbolic, and the instincts inside us are old, precise, and physical. When those instincts are triggered without resolution, we spiral into incoherence. A threat-response system evolved for real danger is now firing in simulated hierarchies with no outlet. The body prepares to fight when there's nothing to engage with.

Social media fuels this system. Every post we make, every like we receive or don't, feeds into our subconscious rank calculations. Most of us aren't celebrities. We're not even mildly "influential." So, when our brains compare our social signals (likes, follows, comments) with those of people who appear higher in the digital hierarchy, it quietly erodes our sense of place. This isn't a rational failure, as some might intone; it's biological, rooted in the same ancient circuitry that once helped us survive on the savannah.

This brings us to an interesting aside about the term "influencer." Most of us believe influencers are precisely that: individuals who have a significant impact on others. This is the core of "influencer marketing," where you hire a person with considerable influence to promote your product and leverage that influence among their followers. What people miss in this formula is that the influencer is not the one doing the influencing; it is the other way around. People with this title are successful due to their visibility and, to a large extent, their social status. The best and most successful personalities on social media don't push the boundaries; they are not the best at leading the conversation into new areas. They are the best at determining where that conversation is already going. Any missteps cause their following to shrink, and they will adjust immediately to return to the expected path. This ties in with our later discussion about the need to be careful with our words, as this linguistic mismatch makes us feel like the people with the least power are the most powerful. When, in fact, they are beholden to a pervasive instinctual mechanic more than most of us.

That exact fight-or-flight mechanism, built for detecting physical threats, is now misfiring in digital space, triggering deep survival instincts where none are needed. A survival system, evolved to assess life-or-death scenarios, now reacts to Instagram as if it were a jungle. The result is confusion, exhaustion, and a constant low-grade sense that we are insufficient. This happens when intellect designs systems severed from the spiral's biological layer.

I've spent a lot of my life trying to live peacefully. I practiced Buddhism, including daily meditation and nonviolence, as well as the rest of the framework, in college. I sincerely believe that anger isn't something to act on.

Then one night at a party, a guy I knew stormed into my house aggressively, loud, posturing, and confrontational. Before I even registered what was happening, I grabbed him by the shirt collar and slammed him into the wall. I didn't think. I didn't plan. It wasn't a choice. My body just moved. I remember the silence that followed more than the slam itself.

People froze. I froze. He backed off, and I stood there stunned, not just by the violence but by how absent I had been from it.

That's the part we don't like to admit. I knew this person. I had no real reason to feel unsafe. But the ancient wiring kicked in anyway. The part of me that meditates and reflects didn't get a vote.

That night didn't destroy my beliefs, but it revealed how fragile belief can be when instinct takes the wheel. It showed me something the spiral demands we understand: any philosophy worth holding must account for the architecture beneath it. If your system collapses under pressure, it is never fully sustainable.

EXPANDING THE RANGE OF THE POSSIBLE

No human has ever acted outside the bounds of human capacity. Given the right conditions and thoughts, we could arrive at any behavior and believe we're justified. That includes everything from genocide to martyrdom, from cruelty to compassion. Every action we've witnessed or imagined is part of what it means to be human.

With each new generation, we expand that capacity. More people, ideas, and interactions all add to the growing catalog of our species' capabilities. We don't, can't, and will never transcend animal behavior; we widen its range. But with that widening comes a new layer of possibility: the capacity to notice what we're doing, to become aware of the patterns shaping us.

Instincts aren't conscious maps. They function like pre-installed overlays on the world. Evolution draws them. They don't ask for our interpretation; they act. But humans are unique in one crucial way: we can see the map and notice the overlay. We can also choose whether to follow, override, or redraw it.

That's what it means to evolve as a species, not just to develop new tools, but to weave experience into recursive awareness. It's not that one of us becomes divine; our species becomes more complete.

Teilhard de Chardin, a French Jesuit priest and paleontologist, referred to this as the Omega Point: a theoretical future state where human consciousness and complexity converge to form a unified awareness, encompassing the totality of experience and being. This is the moment when complexity doesn't just build systems, it reflects on being itself.

A member of the species *Homo sapiens sapiens* who has been "domesticated", as all readers of this book have (and its writer), likely has a familiar skill set: driving a car, reading and writing, cooking food, and speaking a language. These abilities mark the blurry dividing line between us and the "primitive" apes we like to reference. People get uncomfortable seeing an ape doing something recognizably human, like driving a car. Not because it's impossible, but because it threatens the neat category boundary we use to separate "us" from "them."

Even small behaviors unsettle us. When an ape grooms a human, we flinch, not out of fear but of recognition. We see something tender, social, and hygienic, which **feels** human. And that closeness is more disruptive to our identity than any difference could ever be.

But what we call domestication is just instinct management. We build rituals, habits, and social norms that help regulate the raw survival systems still operating under the hood. Driving a car isn't just a skill. It's one of many rituals that act as societal overlays: designed, inherited, and rarely examined.

These are spiral scaffolds, or designed forms, placed over

instinct. Cooking, language, traffic laws, and rituals are all engineered to modulate biological drives. Driving is not a neutral task. It's a symbol of suppressed impulse. You're hurtling a metal box through space at lethal speed, and yet the rules of the road prevent chaos (most of the time). Cooking transforms raw, instinct-driven hunger into something structured, chosen, even aesthetic.

People consider these as upgrades or improvements, but they're just layers. Cultural overlays (map-making strategies) enable us to coexist by organizing and refining the animal urges we still carry. Each of these layers reflects a deeper pattern: coherence built through the acknowledgement, not denial, of the animal beneath.

So when we're unsettled by a non-human animal acting "like us," we're reacting to the fragility of our control systems. If an ape can drive, maybe we're not as fundamentally different as we thought, and maybe our maps are thinner than we'd like to admit.

We often imagine human evolution as the pinnacle of life on Earth. But that's a misunderstanding. We, maybe, are *a* pinnacle, one expression of evolutionary possibility, not *the* pinnacle itself. Every species alive today represents a success story. Our self-awareness doesn't exempt us from the rest of nature. It just adds another layer to it.

Humans have an incredible capacity for tool use and projecting into the future. We're one of the few animals that can predict the movement of something unseen and act accordingly, throwing a spear ahead of a running animal, designing a shelter for a storm that hasn't arrived yet. This capacity helped separate us and allowed us to rise to the position where we are now. But in almost every physical domain, be it strength, sight, smell, or hearing, we are outperformed by other species. Our advantage is almost entirely mental.

Because of this, we tend to assume our conscious minds are always in charge. But often, they're just passengers. Temporarily holding the wheel while taking orders from older forces that steer the direction of the entire world. Instinct, environment, and culture still drive us, even when we think we're choosing freely. These layers take turns leading. The spiral is not always top-down.

What sets us apart is not just that we think, but that we build structures for thought. We shape stories, language, and symbols. We form belief systems and worldviews. We create mental maps and information architecture, attempting to name the territory of reality. These maps let us coordinate, imagine, and design. They liberate us and, simultaneously, often confine us.

Every map reveals and conceals. And the moment we believe the map is the territory, we lose the very freedom that the map was meant to provide.

This is the risk of intellect: it forgets the body it was built on.

Next, we examine how these maps are created and what they do to us once they have been made.

CHAPTER 2

THE MAPMAKER'S MIND

THE SECOND LAYER

She sang songs no bird could keep,
each thread tied bound thought to sleep.
She swept ash of brief-born flame,
as if forgetting were her name.

I f we were only instinct, we'd be predictable animals, reacting automatically to our environments. We're not. Humans have a strange and powerful addition to this system. We can step back, reflect, imagine, and question the very drives that animate us. We don't just react to the world. We map it.

This mapping ability, our capacity to form internal models of reality, gives rise to consciousness. We use language, memory, logic, and imagination to build structures that represent the world. These models allow us to design, coordinate, and cooperate. But they also distort. They overwrite raw signals from instinct with symbols and beliefs. They can trap us in the very maps we use to navigate.

Every belief system (laws, religions, cultural norms) begins this way: as a map. To help frame the shift from raw instinct to symbolic thought, I would like to borrow a distinction from Robert Pirsig, whose work has heavily influenced this book. In *Zen and the Art of Motorcycle Maintenance* and *Lila*, he argued that experience is not composed of matter or of ideas, but of quality. And that quality comes in two forms.

Dynamic quality is the edge of reality. The raw, unfiltered present. Wordless. Improvised. It's what Pirsig called the front of the train, where reality is still being made.

Static quality is everything that sticks: habits, names, instincts, rituals, and systems. It is what we build to hold experience after the fact. It is the map.

One of the interesting aspects of this concept is that the static form of quality is emergent; it arises from the dynamic quality, and in Robert Pirsig's work, this was his central point. Life is not actually dualistic; it arises from a singular entity that he calls the dynamic quality. I have spent years contemplating this, and it closely aligns with many mystical frameworks, such as those found in Buddhist beliefs, the Tao Te Ching, and

Christian thought. The only major flaw I have discovered in this thinking is that it equates dynamic quality and static quality, implying there are two, which immediately returns to dualistic thinking. Of course, this is natural; our experience is dualistic. There are objects that we perceive as subjects, and we are perceived as objects by other subjects. So we shouldn't try to deny this; we should contain it.

I have developed a system to accomplish this because dynamic quality remains singular; it is the bleeding edge of all interaction. Static quality, the emergent layer, is forming different kinds of structures. In my framework, those forms of quality emerge in layers:

- The inorganic gives rise to the biological
- The biological gives rise to the social
- The social gives rise to the intellectual

Each layer emerges from the one before it. And each remains obligated to what gave it life.

That's the spiral. Not a ladder. Not a hierarchy. A recursive stack. Our minds do not float above biology, detached. They sit on it, enmeshed. To evolve consciously, we must see the whole structure and build systems that don't sever their foundations.

This chapter marks the beginning of the second layer of the spiral. It explores how humans construct internal maps, how language, memory, and belief influence perception, and how these symbolic tools can lead us into incoherence when mistaken for reality.

The goal isn't to abandon maps. It's to understand their limits. Without that awareness, we confuse simulation for substance and act with certainty inside fiction.

The danger is built into the strength. Our maps are so precise that we stop seeing them as maps. We feed our instincts not with the world itself, but with our simulation of it. Survival systems, built to react to physical threats, are now triggered by symbols: reputational harm, social exclusion, and narrative loss.

A system evolved for physical danger now lives inside a symbolic environment. It fires in response to ideas. And it doesn't know the difference.

We call that modernity. But spiral distortion is a mismatch between the map layer and the body that built it.

Because our mapping systems operate unconsciously, we often fail to notice them. That's what makes them powerful and dangerous. We don't stop to verify them against reality. We trust them and act on them without hesitation.

The better the map, or the more deeply held it is, the more invisible it becomes. Trust becomes dangerous the moment we forget that all maps are compressions. Every compression loses something. Every symbol conceals as much as it reveals.

Whatever a person encounters will be shaped by the tint of their internal map. Even if they don't know it, that map determines what feels possible, threatening, meaningful, or "real". Once the map becomes conscious, we can ask what's there and what was only drawn in.

In this book, we don't just mean the physical when discussing what is "real". We mean what has an effect: ghosts, gods, emotions, memories. It is real enough if it alters how someone moves through the world. And that reality matters.

We'll refine this definition later. For now, let "real" mean anything that exerts force on behavior.

Once we become aware of the map we're using, we can do two things: try out other maps to test alignment and redraw our own to more accurately reflect what is there.

To do either, we must understand how mapping works, how models form and evolve, and how they betray us when we forget they were never the world.

MAPPING MECHANISMS OF THE CONSCIOUS ANIMAL

Our ability to model reality in our minds lets us be intentional when we build tools, cities, technologies, and social structures. In other words, we reshape our surroundings; layers of the spiral that came before the intellectual. However, this has a strange consequence: we are reshaping the layers of the world that gave rise to us, and thus, they reshape us in return. A city, a classroom, a platform; each one loops back, rewiring instinct and perception, often in ways we never intended.

Many animals have sophisticated mapping systems. Predatory species evolve sensory organs tuned to detect trajectories and timing, optimized to track and intercept prey at its moment of weakness. Prey species evolve different systems entirely. Their perception maps are tuned to movement, threat, and escape. They build models of the world not for conquest, but for survival.

These maps are accurate. But what they highlight is different. A rabbit and a lion can stand in the same field and inhabit entirely different versions. What the rabbit calls safe, a place with wide visibility and no shelter, is a spot a lion would avoid. Every animal's sense of safety is shaped by the map it builds, and every map is shaped by the organs that built it.

Humans evolved a different strategy. We don't lead in smell, sight, sound, or speed. We aren't the best at any single sense. But we're competent in all of them at once. What we lack in specialization, we compensate for in synthesis. Our strength is in how we combine all our systems. We can actively simulate the world around us to a sufficient degree of accuracy.

That simulation doesn't end at the body. It extends into what we build.

Once the environment becomes simulated (digital, symbolic, and architectural) and feeds our instincts with artificial signals, we achieve the separation we discussed in the previous chapter. We feel reputational harm as a danger, respond to crowd dynamics as threat calculus, and sense algorithmic pressure as if it were biological.

This separates the human mapping system from that of every other animal: ours spills outward into our environment, then loops inward to alter the instincts it was built upon.

That's not a metaphor. That's the structure of the spiral.

In *Science and Sanity*, Alfred Korzybski described a uniquely human trait: **time-binding**, the ability to pass thoughts, discoveries, and experiences forward through language, memory, and culture. Each generation inherits the maps of the last, and reshapes them. He believed this capacity could double human knowledge every generation.

I don't think the mechanism is that clean, but the effect is undeniable. Human beings don't just learn. We stack. We absorb others' experiences. We store and reshape them before transmitting them to others. While other species have begun showing signs of this (monkeys in Asia, dolphins in the Gulf), they have not yet turned it into architecture.

What makes us unique isn't just that we have language. It's that language became our **primary mapping tool**. It didn't start that way. It likely evolved as a simple method for passing information about the physical world. But over time, the very idea of what could be *real* expanded. We used language to name the invisible: laws, gods, moods, markets. And as we named them, we began to live inside them.

With sufficient complexity, words stop merely describing reality and begin to **create it.**

Language lets us construct entire worlds before they exist. A skyscraper, a nation, a religion, all built first in the mind, through symbolic scaffolding. An author can describe a landscape you've never seen; your brain will make it as if you've been there. This was the very core of some of our greatest literary works, such as *The Giver* and *Gilgamesh*.

To understand how humans map meaning, we can't treat language as a neutral tool. It's a lens. It shapes what we see, and thus what we ignore; inevitably, it also shapes what we believe is possible.

Before language, there was sensory stacking. Sight, sound, touch, smell; these combine into first-layer maps. What something looks like, how it sounds, or feels, becomes an embedded pattern. "This cup looks like glass, but doesn't feel like it?" "This floor feels warm; maybe it's heated." "You sound calm, but are fidgeting. What's wrong?"

These perceptions become compressed into early meaning, not "glass" or "warm," but a gradient from "safe" or "threatening." They steer us through the world rather than describe it, and with that steering comes distortion.

We rarely recognize that this form of mapping is already **non-Aristotelian.** We're not dealing in clear categories, but in properties and patterns. Most of us are raised in binary frames: true or false, good or bad, hot or cold. But life doesn't work like that. General Semantics, also developed by Korzybski, emphasizes that all labeling is a form of abstraction. The label is never the thing. And strict binaries erase nuance.

Instead of saying "water is hot," we need to learn to ask: "Hot compared to what? To whom? Under what conditions?"

This opens up a spectrum view of reality. A behavior can be both kind and manipulative. A person can be strong and afraid.

A memory can bring grief and comfort. The map becomes thicker, not truer, but more adaptable.

Next comes **memory**, especially the memory of sensory-emotional experiences. Touch something hot, feel pain, remember. Later, the smell of scorched metal might trigger caution. Pain becomes encoded. Danger is inferred, and the map updates.

Language refines this memory. We don't just remember that something hurt. We name it, explain it, and warn others. This shared symbolic memory lets us inherit danger without directly experiencing it. Through stories, it even enables us to inherit *emotion*.

Once basic experiences are stored in memory and shaped by language, we assign **connotations**. Some sensations feel good, others bad. These value judgments reinforce the map. They loop back, altering our sense of what to seek, avoid, or trust.

The sound might bring comfort if your first encounter with thunder happened during a warm, safe night. If it happened during a traumatic storm, it might trigger anxiety. The sound remains the same, but the meaning changes.

This is the beginning of what I call **personal metaphysics**: the ideas, judgments, and associations that sink so deep into the map that they stop feeling like ideas and become as physical as anything else.

The mapping system generates our personal metaphysics. We shape language, culture, religion, traumas, landscapes, and fears. But once built, those maps also shape how we interpret every new experience.

This loop never ends. As babies, our 'metaphysics' was unknowing. As adults, it becomes a patterned, narrowed, and compressed view. Each experience molds it further, and every new concept adds weight to it.

Before we leave the symbolic layer, we need to understand what these mapping systems are made of. Not as tools, as lenses. They shape what enters, stays, and gets encoded.

Next, we look at those parts in detail, including map-making mechanisms and what happens when those maps are calcified.

∼

SENSES AS MAPS

We might believe that our senses are inputs from the world around us. That something we hear is that sound, and that's how it is, no other way of existing. This is a fallacy produced by the subconscious nature of these sensory mapping mechanisms. A sound is perceived by a human the way it is because of our ears' sensory range, the shape of the ears, and the eardrum itself. What we perceive as a step (a whole tonal increment) in music is a 12.2% increase of the previous frequency, which means what we hear as solid intervals constantly gets larger the higher the frequency. This ratio is entirely based on the physical structure of our ear and eardrum. This means that if your ear were shaped like a dog's, a cat's, or any other animal's, our entire idea of sound would be drastically different, and we currently have no way of perceiving what that would be like. So our "map" of sound is one-sided, only our perception of it, and isn't the actual sound at all.

This is the same with all our senses. The things we see are simply different photons being processed by the optic nerve to create an image. The world could look nothing like we perceive it to be, and quite frankly, it probably doesn't. Thus, these senses are only biologically created images, feelings, or sounds that model the world around them, and are not the actual objects or interactions.

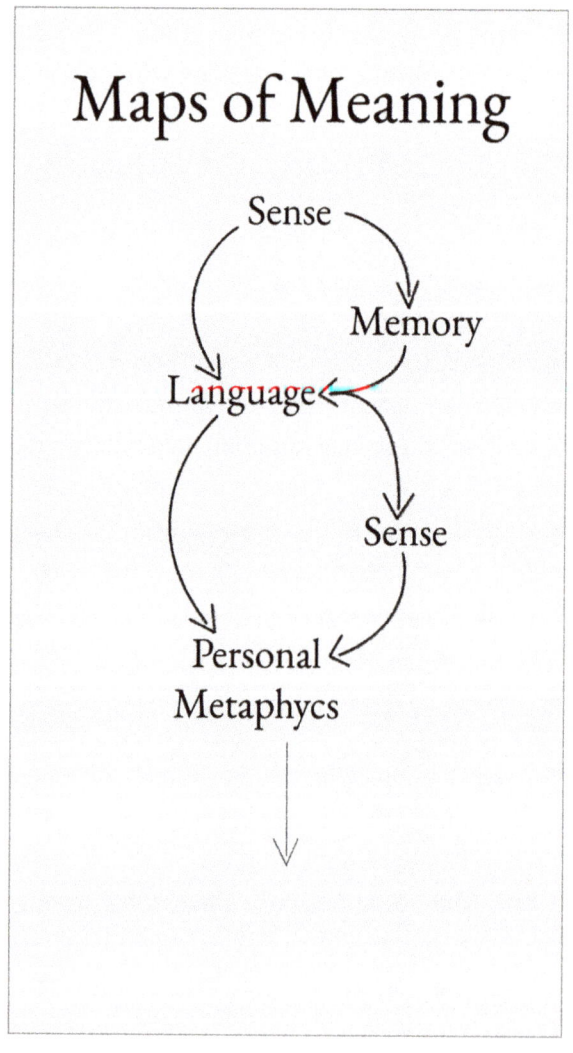

MEMORIES AS MAPS

Memories are not recordings. They are reconstructions, selective and shaped by meaning. We don't remember events as they happen; we remember the impressions they left, the emotional residues, the fragments that mattered most to us at the time. The rest fades, distorts, or is filled in later to create a sense of continuity.

Take childbirth, for example. For some, the memory includes the pain—acute, unforgettable, even traumatic. For others, what endures most vividly is the moment of connection: the arrival of a child, the breath after the storm. This isn't about forgetting pain or pretending it didn't happen. It's the mind's way of prioritizing meaning. We don't relive every sensation; we relive what matters most. That priority is what draws the map.

In this way, memories act like cartographic tools. We chart the terrain of our lives by anchoring to emotional landmarks: moments of joy, sorrow, revelation, rupture. But like any map, the result isn't the whole territory. It's a partial rendering, built from what we noticed, what we cared about, and what we could make sense of. And when a stretch of experience doesn't quite cohere, when our existing beliefs or frameworks can't explain it, we often invent connecting pieces. The brain draws lines between known points, filling the blank space with assumptions.

This is where false memories arise. They aren't really "lies" in the traditional sense; they are more narrative glue. When we recall a difficult conversation or a confusing encounter, we're often patching together an internal logic: "If she said that, and then she walked away, she must have been angry." We don't know she was angry; we inferred it based on past interactions and familiar emotional patterns. It's like trying to draw the middle of the United States based only on detailed maps of the East and West Coasts. Our minds build the middle, not from direct experience, but from contextual guesses. Once the logic behind these contextualized guesses fades due to time or inattention, we almost always only remember the guess, and it slowly solidifies until the perceived difference between the real memory and the contextual guess is no longer discernible.

This process can be helpful. It allows us to navigate life with partial information. But it can also be dangerous. When we confuse inference with truth and believe the filled-in parts of the map as confidently as the parts we actually walked, we risk mistaking fiction for fact. This can damage relationships, fuel anxiety, and entrench distorted self-perceptions.

The goal isn't to stop the mind from mapping; that's impossible. The mind is a meaning-making engine. But we can learn to hold our maps more lightly, to question the parts drawn in haste or fear, and to notice the difference between the landmarks we lived and the filler we created to make sense of it all.

Some have described depression as a kind of perceptual collapse, a narrowing of attention. The present fades. The map takes over. Rather than sensing the world as it is, the mind loops through memory, reanimating old pain until it feels indistinguishable from the now. The body follows, reliving sensations that no longer belong to the moment.

This loop can be disrupted by returning to the body, focusing on your breath, the floor, the wind, or placing a hand on your chest. These small anchors pull us back into contact with the world. Over time, they soften the memory's grip, turning it from something we inhabit into something we carry —a story, not a place. A contour on the map is no longer mistaken for the terrain.

This ability to transform experience into abstraction is one of memory's essential functions. We're not designed to remember every detail. We're built to extract patterns or shapes. This is part of the power behind "the map is not the territory": the distance between the two allows us to step back, to compress the noise of experience into a form we can use. For most of us, that abstraction is a gift. It allows healing. It allows clarity. It enables the past to become past.

But for those whose memory is too precise, this abstraction doesn't happen. Some have written about the strange burden of total recall, how the inability to forget detail can trap a person in endless reliving, unable to form the wider shapes that meaning requires. Without distance, there is no map. Without a map, you cannot stand above the terrain and know where you are.

This awareness doesn't guarantee clarity, but it gives us the distance we need to navigate. Not all memories are meant to be relived. Some are intended to be transformed. Turned into story, wisdom, direction; into maps we can walk with, rather than drown in. But memories don't just sit passively; they seek shape. And language gives them one.

LANGUAGES AS MAPS

Language offers a fascinating insight into the world of human understanding. The evolution that occurs during every generation, the way words take on new meanings as concepts change in society, and the evolution of what is considered proper in each language are fantastic examples of how language is intrinsically connected with our perception and understanding of the world around us. However, it is also undeniable and straightforward that it does not refer to the world it claims to.

As said earlier, a good author can paint you a picture of a place you have never seen, and you can conjure the image of that place in your mind with fantastic precision and skill. But the words used to convey that image are not the image or the place referred to. They symbolise the concepts and ideas lurking in our minds that cannot be vocalized.

Nobody has ever spoken directly to another mind; they have only sent outputs across to be processed into a new map by the receiver of the sounds. When I say 'table,' I am referring to an object that we all know is symbolized by that word, but the object is not the word. You cannot put plates on that word.

NON-ARISTOTELIAN MAPPING

Language is one of the most powerful tools in our mapping system. However, to understand what it does and doesn't, we must consider what we've been discussing: **the map is not the territory.**

Maps simplify. They flatten. They leave things out so we can carry something useful. That's what language does with reality. It packages form into a symbol, complexity into a phrase. And that's where the distortion begins, because how we label things shapes how we relate to them. We don't just describe the world; we filter it.

This is where **non-Aristotelian logic** becomes essential. In classical Aristotelian thinking, things are binary: either in front or behind, hot or cold, and so on. But in the physical world, almost nothing fits those clean categories. Temperature lies on a continuum. Location depends on perspective. Emotions blend. Behavior overlaps.

Non-Aristotelian logic teaches us that labels are never the whole picture; they're tools of approximation. They help us function, and that's all.

Let's name the structure we're working with:
• Language is connected to the physical world.
• But words are not the things they describe.

• Language is a way of representing physical experience in non-physical space.

That distance between symbol and thing isn't a flaw. It's what allows for *abstraction*, and abstraction is what gives us freedom of thought.

That's the power of symbolic thinking: it allows us to operate on gradients, imagine possibilities, and generalize across specificity. And that abstraction, paradoxically, gets us *closer to*, not *farther from,* truth. It reveals the underlying structure rather than being distracted by details. And when those abstractions are shared, repeated, ritualized, and embedded, they cease to be tools for thought. They become the scaffolding of worldviews.

If language were the territory and perfectly mirrored reality, we wouldn't be able to think in this way. No general terms, categories, ambiguity, metaphors, or progress would exist.

Language helps us climb out of immediacy. It allows us to guess, revise, and consider multiple frames. It gives us both specificity and ambiguity, continuity and nuance. It lets us test reality without being crushed by its weight. Without that ability, we'd be stuck in what is. With it, we can explore what's possible.

We've explored how individuals form internal maps, how instinct and environment shape perception, and how meaning emerges through layers of attention. But maps don't just live in people. When shared across time and community, they solidify into something bigger: belief systems, which become the scaffolding for law, ritual, morality, even reality itself. And when those shared maps begin to break down or evolve, the systems we live inside shift with them.

CHAPTER 3

WORLDS WE INHERIT AND BUILD

THE THIRD LAYER

Every elder spoke one word:
"Craft upholds the weight it stirred."
Go far," they said, "wanting ends."
She bore the heat her making sends.

This moment in human evolution represents something unusual and perhaps even unprecedented. For most of evolutionary history, survival was shaped by the physical: sharper claws, stronger muscles, better camouflage. That still plays a role today, but is no longer the main driver for us. What now determines human survival is social, cultural, and conceptual. This can probably be most easily seen by how resilient our food systems are; most people who will read this book have never **truly** been hungry and have almost definitely never faced a famine. The only frequent causes of actual famine in the modern world are brought on by ourselves. War and corruption are among the primary factors that can destabilize our extensive trade and food networks. Less than a few hundred years ago, this wasn't the case. Loss of a few degrees from global temperatures, or a swarm of locusts at the wrong time of year, could send an entire region into famine conditions in the blink of an eye. Even back then, we relied on cultural and social connections to mitigate the impact of this physical environment on our survival, but they weren't as robust as they are today. Our mapping mechanisms are now our primary drivers for evolutionary selection.

As we've discussed, we are not governed solely by their instincts. We model the world, reflect on our behavior, and reshape our conditions. That ability gives us something evolution has never seen before: metaphysical self-responsibility. We are no longer just shaped by our environment; we shape it. This mapping ability is an unbelievably strong evolutionary advantage. Because we can proactively and intentionally change the physical environment, we can make almost any aspect of our existence advantageous. We can find a proper function for a vast, muscular bodybuilder, just as we can find a use for the scrawny brainiac (to be overly simplistic). This feature of our capabilities has led to the incredible expansion of human dominance over the last few thousand years, which, from an evolutionary perspective, is a relatively short period for a species to spread as rapidly as we have. One thing we often overlook is that, although we intentionally shape our environment, the effect of this altered environment on us is rarely considered.

This seems quite simple in concept: the environment shapes us, we shape the environment, and then the environment shapes us again. Of course, this cycle exists. However, we rarely discuss how that middle step affects the environment's impact on us; we often see ourselves as passive bystanders to evolution, rather than as the primary drivers.

Despite our scientific advances, we still do not understand how evolution functions in complex environments. We can edit genes, but struggle to explain how traits stabilize across generations, even in response to physical inputs, let alone to pressures like status, identity, or belief. Yet we intuitively grasp symbolic meaning. Myths, metaphors, ideologies, and visions of destiny aren't side effects of being human. They are the language we have slowly built to understand just how we shape the future, and how it shapes us. We can observe this phenomenon dating back thousands of years, with evidence to support it. The very structure of the Epic of Gilgamesh, which is believed to have been originally composed around 2100 BC, is centered on this phenomenon. The epic is structured to show how stories shape us, and then how we become the formers of those very stories, a transition that is likened to becoming immortal within the epic. The stories in many creation myths tell how human-like "gods" formed the world that gave rise to us. In my opinion, these myths, stories, and beliefs are now the primary drivers of human evolution.

MAPS TO METAPHYSICS

In earlier eras, metaphysical beliefs weren't central to survival. One could believe the world rested on turtles or was held up by giants without affecting their hunt or harvest. But that's no longer true. Today, we go to war for flags, identities, and imagined orders, things with no physical form, yet immense consequence. If reality is defined by what governs behavior, then the metaphysical has become more real than the physical world itself.

That shift can feel disorienting. We still want reality to be solid, measurable, and undeniably true. *I* still wish for this, and at one point in my life, I believed in an undeniable "reality"; however, *physical reality* was never the whole story. Even among animals, intangible factors such as chance, the ability to repeat successful actions, social hierarchy, and intellectual capacity have long shaped outcomes as much as strength or speed. We inherited that layering. Our rituals, etiquette, and status games are extensions of those ancient dynamics.

When immediate threats, such as starvation or predation, fade, the challenge shifts elsewhere. For modern humans, it has moved into belief. Our survival now depends on the systems, stories, and identities we construct, and how well they enable us to coexist. That sounds precarious, but it also opens a new kind of agency; we can participate in evolution. We build tools. We shape environments. We create meaning.

This doesn't mean we should abandon skepticism or caution. But it does mean we shouldn't panic. The same evolutionary intelligence that brought us this far, through tooth, fire, language, and law, is still unfolding. If we can learn to see it clearly and steer it consciously, we may not be evolving away from our animal nature, but toward a more integrated and self-aware form of it. And if the metaphysical has become our new terrain, then the belief systems that shape it are not background, they're blueprint.

However, before we turn to how these belief systems evolve and break down, I want to pause and name one story about this moment that I do not believe is true.

THE HUMAN WAS NEVER SINGULAR

On Posthumanism, and Why I Don't Buy It

There's a growing school of thought, philosophical, technological, sometimes aesthetic, known as posthumanism. It argues that we've passed beyond the era of the human as central to meaning, ethics, or design. In this view, agency now belongs to systems: artificial intelligence, digital platforms, and climate feedback loops. The individual human subject is no longer the locus of will or consequence, but one node among many: interchangeable, interwoven, and ultimately unstable.

Some of that critique is valid. The autonomous, self-determining individual was always a myth of privilege. No one exists outside a system. No one acts alone. Our languages are borrowed. Even our bodies are ecological collaborations, with more bacteria than bone. I agree with that, but I disagree with what gets claimed next.

Posthumanism tends to suggest that because we are enmeshed, we are no longer ourselves, that because we are shaped, we do not shape, and that because we are distributed, we are dissolved. But this framing trades one mistake for another. It replaces the fiction of sovereignty with the fiction of disappearance. It forgets that we are not just nodes; we actively participate, and participation implies attention.

My disagreement isn't only metaphysical, but heavily ethical. When responsibility is distributed across systems, it becomes easy to believe no one is accountable. Design becomes directionless, and change is accidental. However, even in a networked world, awareness remains crucial. Agency may be partial, but it is real. And responsibility begins with this attention: our capacity to notice, name, and respond to the systems we're inside.

There's also a strange ahistoricism to much of posthuman discourse. The idea that human identity is porous, contingent, and emergent isn't new. Indigenous cosmologies have said for thousands of years that humans are not separate from animals, rivers, or stars. A vast array of creation myths has humans **literally emerging** from clay or sea foam, and mystical traditions have long taught that the self is both authentic and relational. The self exists, just not alone. Posthumanism often presents itself as if it has uncovered something radical, when in fact it is merely rephrasing something ancient.

On a linguistic/semantic level, I reject the framing that there ever was a cleanly human era, now passed. We have never been singular. We have always been ourselves within systems: biological, ecological, cultural, and symbolic. The idea that we are now "posthuman" assumes a coherence we never had and a rupture that hasn't occurred.

A better question is whether we are finally beginning to understand what it has meant to be all along. To be is not to be alone at the top of a pyramid; it is to be a localized expression of something layered, recursive, and real. It is to be a boundary and a bridge. It is to be part of a whole and yet remain singular.

Even rocks have individuality. They sit. They shape. They wear down mountains and hold heat through the night. They are both selves and systems, both matter and meaning. So are we.

If posthumanism helps us remember our embeddedness, that's good. But if it invites us to forget that attention still matters, that coherence still matters, and that care still matters, then I want something else.

Not a return to human exceptionalism, nor a leap into posthuman abstraction. Something older, and maybe more precise.

A practiced being-hood.

That's what we've always been. Beings, not just humans. Not isolated and not special. Interacting, perceiving, and altering the field through participation. The failure wasn't in the condition; it was in the language. We didn't have the awareness to develop a way to accurately name what we were.

Now we do.

And that's where Olamic speech begins:

Not by redefining the world, but by finally learning to talk about the one we've always been inside.

BREAKDOWN OF STANDING BELIEF SYSTEMS

Since we live inside systems shaped by belief more than by biology, we need to understand those beliefs, study them like we do any physical aspect of ourselves. We need to examine where they come from, how they work, and what they've become. Humans have been mapping meaning for thousands of years. We've always needed a framework to organize the unknown, to pass down wisdom, and to situate ourselves inside a larger story. And while language allows us to share individual thoughts and experiences, religion appears to be the earliest form of metaphysics for the scaffolding of our shared mental world.

These are the architectural and infrastructural components of these systems. The stories we believe about gods, order, justice, destiny, and so much more form the underlying maps we use to interpret life. They shape how we treat each other, explain the past, and shape our imagination of the future. And they've continually evolved to reflect the needs and pressures of the world they emerge from.

METAPHYSICS AS MAPPING

Across time and culture, religions have sought to explain the deep structure of the world; not just its surface events, but its hidden order. The ancient Greeks believed in a pantheon of gods that we now encounter as mythology. At the time, these were not quaint stories but living systems of meaning —the stories of Olympus oriented Greek life. By projecting qualities onto divine figures, the Greeks created a framework for interpreting the world: organizing chaos into something navigable. Appease the gods, fulfill your obligations, and perhaps the world would align. And if tragedies engulfed everything, maybe the gods were at odds. These stories offered hope and direction. Daily goals were woven into cosmic structure.

In this sense, science is not the opposite of religion but a sibling. It, too, attempts to explain how the world works. It seeks not divine intention but mechanical law; replicable cause rather than narrative coherence. Yet it functions similarly by providing a map. And like any map, it is vulnerable to becoming brittle. When a metaphysical frame (scientific or spiritual) is held too tightly, it can start to exclude what does not fit. Data that contradicts our expectations is resisted. We fail to adapt. Belief becomes boundary.

This is not a flaw of science specifically; science explicitly tries to resist this in its methods. It is, instead, a feature of belief itself. Once a worldview has structured enough experience, it becomes resistant to restructuring. Even brilliant systems can ossify. A belief held long enough becomes a filter for what is allowed to enter the mind, a way to conserve order. But what was once a strength becomes a limitation. New experiences cannot always find a place. The system, built to understand reality, now struggles to incorporate it.

This is why the relationship between science and religion matters so deeply here. They are not adversaries. They are different languages attempting to describe the same terrain. By embracing both the mystic capacity for insight and the empirical demand for evidence, the map becomes fuller. Mythology gives access to the unseen, the unmeasurable, the intangible. Science helps test, refine, and remain honest. Together, they form a translational bridge: a way to speak of a god while speaking of gravity—not a contradiction, but a convergence, two vocabularies for the same mystery.

A striking illustration of the relationship between myth, perception, and reality can be seen in the year 536 AD, when multiple historical records describe the sun dimming or disappearing for over a year. These accounts were long dismissed. The same texts describe demons abducting children and cosmic punishment; it was easy for 19th- and 20th-century scholars to dismiss the "vanished sun" as one more superstition in an age of magical thinking.

But the modern scientific record will not let those accounts go. Ice cores from Greenland and the Arctic show a massive volcanic eruption in 536, likely in Iceland, followed by another in 541 near the tropics. The amount of ash and sulfate entering the atmosphere would have transformed daylight across much of the northern hemisphere. Anyone who has lived through heavy wildfire smoke has seen how particulate matter can make the sun dim enough to be visible only indirectly. Scale that up by an order of magnitude, and the sky would take on an otherworldly pall. The sun may not have "disappeared" in the literal sense these writers imagined, but their map (mythic, symbolic, metaphysical) was preserving a real event beneath layers of interpretation.

This is the key point: when myth is discarded because its explanations feel primitive, the data embedded within it is often discarded as well. Ancient writers did not have the conceptual tools to distinguish between "metaphysics" and "empirical fact" as later thinkers do. Their language compressed experience into the symbolic. Ours compresses it into the scientific. Both are maps. Both distort but also preserve.

What matters here is the mechanism, not the vocabulary. Mythic explanations name forces in the only language available to the people describing them. The map was inaccurate in reason, but accurate in experience. The event happened. Their world dimmed. They suffered. And they reached for the interpretive tools they had.

Even the way we date that year carries its own metaphysics. "536 AD" is not a neutral label. AD, meaning *Anno Domini*, "in the year of the Lord", was devised by monks whose worldview was explicitly Christian. CE ("Common Era") attempts to secularize the same timeline, but it does not change the point around which the system is built. The zero remains the supposed date of Jesus' birth. The names shift, but the metaphysical anchor does not. A genuinely "common" era would require rebuilding the calendar from a shared reference point rather than relabeling a Christian schema as neutral.

This is not an indictment of one system over another. It serves as a reminder that maps reflect the values and viewpoints of their creators. Even our calendars carry metaphysics.

To drive this point home, consider another case where myth and superstition appear to lead us straight into empirical truth. In Ireland stands a megalithic structure called Newgrange, also known as Brú na Bóinne, "the palace of the Bóinne" (Bóinne being the nearby river and the namesake of the goddess Boann). The burials in Newgrange are dated to roughly 5,200 years ago. The passageway into the mound became sealed thousands of years ago and was left largely undisturbed until modern archaeological work.

That work revealed two crucial facts. First, on the winter solstice, the rising sun shines directly into the passage, illuminating the inner chamber. Second, genetic analysis of one of the individuals buried there shows the person was the child of an incestuous union, most likely between close kin such as siblings or parent and child.

From a modern, scientific viewpoint, these are discoveries. Within the mythic frame surrounding Brú na Bóinne, these confirmations are evident. One myth tells that the sun god, Dagda, desired to be with Boann, goddess of the river Bóinne, and so held the sun in the sky to spend a night with her. In this tale, the sun quite literally "penetrates" the mound. This image aligns eerily with the winter solstice light entering a structure long associated with a womb in ancient Irish thought. The myth also says they conceived a child. Brú na Bóinne is, in multiple Irish cycles, related to incestuous unions and tangled kinship.

The passage into Brú na Bóinne had been sealed for millennia when these stories were recorded. Yet the narratives preserve, in symbolic form, information about the site that is empirically true. The myth remembers what the stones and the genes remember.

This should force a reconsideration of the habit of treating mythology as "unreal." Myth is not a failed attempt at science. It is a different compression of reality, tuned to various purposes. At its best, it is a long-term memory system for a culture, a means of encoding events, places, and relationships into stories and symbols so they can survive the erosion of time. When we read myth only as error, we miss the data it carries. When we read science as the only mechanism, we miss the meanings it silently erases. The work here is not to choose one over the other, but to learn to read both, and then to notice where they converge.

THE LANGUAGE OF REALITY

We've said it before: words don't capture reality, they approximate it. The Newgrange myths don't reveal the exact reality of what happened or how it occurred. However, this point bears repeating, as it's foundational. Language doesn't mirror the world; it modulates it. Each word acts as a lens, shaped by culture, history, and personal experience. They filter reality into something we can pass between minds, or through time. Meaning isn't fixed in the symbol. It lives in the space between speaker and listener, context and interpretation.

This is especially true when it comes to metaphysical ideas. The specific language we use, whether we call it God, Source, the Tao, the Void, or Nothingness, is secondary to the quality of the expressed insight. The words themselves are scaffolding. Saying the "wrong" word for the right idea might interfere with someone else's understanding, but it won't necessarily distort your own. The resonance of a metaphysical truth lives in its capacity to orient your being, not just to sound correct.

Because of this linguistic relativity, we can use whatever version of language maps most clearly to our experience. And when we look closely, we find that many belief systems across time and place are saying fundamentally similar things. They employ different metaphors, rituals, and cosmologies, but the underlying currents often converge. They speak to the same longings: for meaning, for belonging, for order, for connection to something greater than ourselves. They are addressed to different kinds of hearts in disparate environments, but the essence is remarkably consistent.

What matters most in our relationship to this symbolic system is that we do not mistake it for the territory. The words are not the truth. They are an attempt to show us something, to orient us within a vast, invisible structure. The danger comes when we believe the map is the thing it describes—when we hold our metaphors too tightly, or confuse symbolic representation with ontological fact.

Language, then, is not a destination. It is a guide. Its job is not to end the search, but to point toward the kinds of questions worth asking. Newgrange is associated with incest, and this association always describes the last usage of Newgrange before the passage collapsed, or the magic was broken. It is a parable, warning people to be wary of this kind of relationship, a story told presumably since the burials took place over 5,000 years ago. And when these stories do their job well, they don't just describe reality but invite us into a deeper relationship with it.

One of the most persistent features of human cognition is its tendency to categorize the world into opposites. Our mental maps categorize reality into binary opposites: mind and body, abstract and concrete, joy and sorrow, and strength and weakness. These oppositions are not intrinsic to the world itself. They are artifacts of perception: simplifications we impose to navigate complexity. But once established, they become powerful. They shape how we interpret our instincts, relate to others, and build systems that reflect and reinforce those divides.

The oldest metaphysical systems, as well as our earliest religions and cosmologies, reflect this tendency. They begin with dualities: light and dark, fire and water, heaven and earth, good and evil. Some traditions eventually expand these into more complex cosmologies, but the foundation remains polarized. This mirrored something tangible in our evolutionary experience. To survive, you had to be fast, not slow; cautious, not reckless; accepted, not cast out. In most mammalian species, you are male or female, with roles defined accordingly. But these categories, while evolutionarily functional, are not exhaustive. They are strategies, not truths. We see this in the natural world: asexual reproduction, fluid behaviors, and cooperative specialization challenge the neatness of binary roles. In this light, division is not a reflection of reality but a mechanism of efficiency. It simplifies the function by isolating responsibility. And evolution, more than anything, rewards what works, whether or not it reflects the fullness of what is.

There is a danger in this that I want to address directly before discussing it further, though, and we can approach this by examining it from yet another old story. Once again, we turn to the Greeks, as we will do frequently, mainly because we have a wealth of ancient Greek writings, but also because of the profound impact these writings have had on the civilizations that evolved into the modern Western world.

This last fact, that Greece was a major influence on Rome, which was a significant influence on almost everywhere (at the height of their power, they ruled from Britain to the Sahara), is precisely what I want to approach right now, as one of the formative stories in Greek mythology is the myth of Pandora.

This is a very "well-known" myth; I put the word known in quotes because while we all know her name, almost none of us know anything about her. We see a lot about her box instead.

This is where things get interesting. In Greek myth, Pandora did not have a box. In the earliest stories, she had nothing. What she had wasn't important; it was what she was: a woman. According to Greek mythology, Pandora was the first woman and marked the end of the age of "man." This happened for various reasons that are convoluted in the mythological stories, but the why isn't what I want to point out right now; what I want to point out is the shifting of the story to support a different metaphysical goal.

The story of Pandora's "thing", which was never a box at first, is definitely old. She is initially depicted without anything, but shortly after her original story, we begin to see stories of her with a jar, which is the progenitor of our modern story of Pandora's Box; however, there is a fundamental difference. Erasmus, a 16th-century writer, is credited with introducing the concept of Pandora's Box and simultaneously "blaming" Pandora for opening it. Previously, the story wasn't one of curiosity or the way women brought evil things into the world; the story was one of the fracturing of a singularity into duality.

The original Greek story states that the world was composed of Titans, Gods, and men (literal humans), and that women did not exist. Prometheus steals fire and gives it to the men, partly so they can worship him properly and burn their sacrifices, and partly for other reasons. Of course, Prometheus is punished for this, but more importantly to the Greeks, it gave rise to the dualistic form that humans take, characterized by the distinction between male and female.

This tendency to divide and to split experience into opposing categories is not unique to humans. It's not even limited to biology. In fact, one of the core insights of modern physics is that what appears separate often arises from something once unified. The divisions we observe between particles, forces, or fields are frequently the result of what physicists call broken symmetry.

The Higgs field offers a striking example. It is the mechanism that gives particles their mass. But mass, in this context, is not a primordial trait. It's a consequence of imbalance; a rupture in a previously uniform state. Before that break, the field was symmetrical, its properties evenly distributed. But once symmetry was broken, difference emerged. Particles became distinct. Form took shape.

A helpful metaphor here is ice. At room temperature, water molecules move freely, with no fixed structure. Their behavior is symmetrical. But when frozen, that fluidity collapses into rigidity. Order appears. The symmetry isn't destroyed, it's concealed beneath the visible form.

We'll explore this concept more fully in *Volume Two*, when we examine how perception, memory, and consciousness interact with symmetry. But for now, the key insight is this: many of our sharpest conceptual boundaries, such as those between self and other, mind and body, good and evil, are not reflections of reality's deepest structure. They are crystallizations—frozen states of something more fluid.

Symmetry, or unity, is the underlying fabric. Difference is a surface effect, one that is beneficial, even necessary, but not ultimate. Recognizing this doesn't render distinctions meaningless. It situates them. It shows us that categories are tools, not truths. And like all tools, their value depends on how and when they're used.

Buddhist metaphysics engages this insight not by denying duality, but by softening it. Through meditative practice, it invites the mind to hold seemingly opposing states simultaneously: to remain while in motion, to act while at rest, to exist without clinging to existence. The aim is not synthesis, but spaciousness and the ability to see opposites as co-arising, not conflicting.

This isn't abstract mysticism. It's a reflection of lived reality. Part of us is always still, carrying continuity, memory, identity. And part of us is constantly moving, spinning with the planet, breathing, changing, evolving. The Buddhist path trains perception to notice this simultaneity. Not to resolve it into one side or the other, as this would collapse the insight. But instead, to dwell in both.

The difficulty, of course, is that traditional practices, especially those that help us transcend binary thought, require time, discipline, and stillness. They were designed for lives paced by the sun and seasons, not the algorithm. The insights remain relevant. But the means of accessing them often feel out of reach. That doesn't make them obsolete. It just means we may need new forms to carry ancient wisdom.

Christianity offers another path through the illusion of separation, one built not only on paradox, but also on incarnation. At the heart of its theology is a claim that defies binary logic: God, though wholly other, became fully human. Divinity did not remain distant. It entered the world, took on flesh, and shared in the limitations of suffering, joy, uncertainty, and death.

This creates a striking tension: you are not God, and yet God is in you. The Holy Spirit is not merely above or beyond; it is described as breath, presence, and indwelling force—the very animation of life.

From a scientific lens, this is less alien than it seems. Evolutionarily, we are made of the same systems that formed stars and cells. Chemically, we carry the dust of ancient galaxies. The structures that made us are not external; they live within us. In this way, the Incarnation can be understood as a metaphor for embeddedness: we are shaped by what we also contain.

But this idea, like many profound ones, is often buried under layers of ritual or doctrine. Its core insight that human and divine are not opposites but co-present can be lost beneath inherited language. If we recover that intention, the Incarnation becomes not just a theological claim but a design pattern, a map for reconciling separation and unity within the structure of being itself.

Hinduism offers a different route, one that does not resolve contradiction but honors it. Rather than insisting on a singular face of divinity, Hinduism simultaneously embraces the many and the one. Its pantheon of gods expresses creation, destruction, wisdom, love, and distinct forms, pointing to a shared source: Brahman.

Brahman is not a god in the Western sense. It is the formless, infinite, unchanging substrate of reality. The gods and stories are portals to this insight. Through multiplicity, the underlying unity is glimpsed. Contradiction is not something to eliminate, but something to incorporate.

This framework reaches its philosophical height in Advaita Vedanta, which teaches that the self (Atman) and Brahman are not-two. What appears to be a separation between subject and object is *maya*: a useful illusion. A mask. One that can guide, but must eventually be set down. Here, Hinduism asks you to live inside a paradox. To rest where distinctions dissolve. To stand in a place beyond either/or.

All these traditions (Buddhist, Christian, Hindu) carry immense intention behind their metaphors. They are not merely sets of beliefs or behavioral codes. They are design languages for perceiving what ordinary speech cannot hold. Across cultures and centuries, specific individuals have experienced states of awareness that transcend dualism—beyond the dichotomies. What they found was not chaos. It was spaciousness. A coherence too significant for categories.

Trying to share that view is not easy. Imagine spending your whole life staring at the side of a mountain, only to turn around and realize you're on a vast overlook. Valleys, rivers, and ridgelines unfold in every direction. The terrain was always there; you couldn't see it.

These teachers, from Jeshua to Siddhartha Gautama or Muhammad, Gandhi, and Thich Nhat Hanh, spoke from that wider view. They used metaphor not to obscure, but to preserve. They understood that if you talk too plainly from that place, you shatter the listener's map. But if you speak symbolically, you can carry someone closer without breaking them.

They were not evading. They were being precise at scale. They wanted to protect the journeyer, but pointed toward the substrate of reality.

Trying to convey that experience to others is incredibly difficult. It's hard to turn to someone and say, "Everything you know is only a tiny fraction of everything there is." Most people don't respond well to that. The mind clings to certainty. That's why, throughout history, those who've seen further have used metaphors, parables, and stories crafted to speak across differing maps of reality, because direct language would have shattered too many assumptions too quickly.

What unites these teachings isn't agreement on cosmology or ethics. It's something more profound: a shared realization that dualism is a kind of useful illusion. While the world seems to be structured in opposites, those opposites often blur at the edges. Although the dualistic frame helps us function in everyday life, it's not a complete picture. The fundamental insight offered by these traditions is not to reject the map, but to see through it. As the Rastafari tradition wisely puts it, the goal is not just to understand but to 'overstand'. To be able, at least sometimes, to step outside the binary lens and perceive the continuity that was always there.

The interesting thing about metaphors is that they mean almost nothing until they are already understood. That might sound paradoxical, but it's what gives metaphor its strange power. It allows someone to express an insight that sounds outlandish until the listener has gone far enough in their own experience for the metaphor to suddenly make sense.

Take the Gnostics, for example, early Christians who believed that God did not dwell in a separate heaven but was embedded in everything: the trees, the soil, the human body, the stars. This belief was drawn directly from the metaphor-laden teachings of Jeshua. He spoke of the kingdom of heaven being "within," likening the divine to leaven in bread or a mustard seed growing in hidden soil. But he spoke this way because saying it directly would have broken too much too fast. And even with that shield of metaphor, it got him killed. Socrates met the same fate by speaking too clearly about meta-physical truth in a society that wasn't ready to hold it. In both cases, the message threatened the structures that made the society feel stable. And when metaphors begin to dissolve those foundations, the instinct is often to silence the speaker.

But there's a deeper point here: metaphors don't transfer cleanly from one person's mind to another. Whoever speaks in metaphor is doing so from inside their own map of reality. And unless the listener has built a map with similar landmarks, the metaphor won't land. No matter how many times it's explained, it will sound vague, abstract, or nonsensical. That's the hidden price of metaphor: it only opens when you're ready to see what it's pointing toward.

This is what secular language often forgets. We tend to believe that if we say something clearly enough, it will be understood. That truth is a matter of precision. But metaphysical insight doesn't work that way. You can't talk someone into a new worldview. You can only walk beside them while their map reshapes itself. Until a person has had the experiences, reflections, or breakdowns that stretch their inner framework, the language of transformation will fall flat or sound like nonsense.

That's why mystical traditions rely on riddles, parables, and puzzles. *Koans* in Zen Buddhism, paradoxical questions used in meditation to break habitual thought patterns, and symbolic teachings in the Kabbalah aren't meant to be solved. They're intended to undo the listener's current way of thinking. "What is the sound of one hand clapping?" "Does a falling tree make a sound if no one hears it?" At first glance, these seem pointless or clever. But they're not. They're disruption tools, designed to short-circuit the binary logic of the conscious mind and force a deeper kind of awareness to emerge.

This might seem like a stretch. How could something so simple unlock the nature of reality? However, remember that, in this framework, reality encompasses anything that impacts the organism. So when you ask, "Did the tree make a sound?" you're really asking: What counts as real? Does an event require a witness? Is perception necessary for existence? What begins as a small crack in language quickly becomes a gateway to vast questions. And to even start answering them, you have to change. Not just your vocabulary, but your being.

AWAKENING THE INTERNAL MIRROR

Humans love to celebrate self-awareness. We're one of the few species to look into a mirror and say, "That's me." This ability, to recognize our own reflection, sets us apart from much of the animal kingdom and marks an essential stage in cognitive development. But we are now beginning to step into something more profound: an awareness not just of our external image, but of our internal one. A capacity to turn inward and ask, "Who is the one doing the looking?"

And this internal image or sense of self we carry is far more significant than the face we recognize in a glass. It shapes our thoughts, relationships, fears, and desires. It's the hidden architecture behind our choices. And for much of human history, we've had little time or space to examine it. The urgency of survival kept our gaze fixed outward on the weather, predators, crops, and conflict. But now, many of us live with just enough distance from those daily threats to begin asking more fundamental questions. Questions not about what we see, but about how we see. About what it means to be.

This shift allows us to explore metaphysical ideas more openly. We are beginning to talk about what happens inside: meaning, pattern, and purpose. And unlike in previous eras, we don't always need a metaphor to do it. We're slowly developing a worldview capable of pointing more directly at the structures within us. It's not always precise, but it's getting clearer.

I believe this emerging capacity has a biological origin. It's what evolution has prepared us for. But its effects are undeniably spiritual. When we start to see ourselves from the inside out, we're not just understanding, we're transcending. We're not just using maps, we're beginning to redraw them, together.

But as we redraw these maps, we also face a deeper question: What material are we mapping? What exactly flows through our experiences before we describe them, explain them, or even name them? The answer isn't just "objects" or "events." It's something more immediate and more challenging to pin down: a sense of rightness, presence, or value in the texture of the moment itself.

This is where we turn to quality.

HOW REALITY ORGANIZES ITSELF AFTER EXPERIENCE

We need a more comprehensive framework for describing reality to understand the origins of our metaphysical systems and how to refine them. I use a model adapted from Robert Pirsig's work, which divides experience into two broad categories: dynamic quality and static quality.

Dynamic quality is the edge of becoming, the immediate, raw, indescribable experience of reality before it's labeled or categorized. It's the flash of insight, the presence of awe, the shift that precedes structure.

Static quality is what happens after: the patterns we recognize, codify, and pass on. Static quality includes everything from atoms to rituals to moral codes. It's how we make dynamic experience stable, repeatable, and communicable.

Static quality expresses itself in four major layers:

- Inorganic quality: the physical world, governed by matter and energy
- Biological quality: life, survival instincts, embodied interaction
- Societal (or cultural) quality: norms, traditions, hierarchies, cooperation
- Intellectual quality: abstraction, reflection, science, philosophy

Each of these layers emerged from the one before it. Intellect emerged from culture, which emerged from life, which emerged from matter. But emergence does not erase responsibility. Each layer is obligated to serve the one that gave it life.

So, our intellect must serve society, not dominate it. Society must serve biology, not suppress or distort it. Biology, in turn, must remain in the right relationship with the physical world that sustains it.

When this spiral of obligation is respected, things thrive. When it's broken, systems collapse. This is evident in climate change, mental health crises, and political alienation. Intellect has broken from its roots. It's generating maps endlessly (abstract systems, plans, ideologies) without checking the terrain they're meant to represent.

INORGANIC QUALITY

Inorganic quality is the domain of matter, energy, gravity, and physical law. This is the oldest form of static quality: the patterns that emerged after the Big Bang as things cooled, slowed, and began to take shape.

At first, there was near-perfect symmetry, an undifferentiated energy field. However, as the universe expanded and cooled, that symmetry was broken. Tiny fluctuations grew. Particles differentiated. Masses formed. The result was structure, not imposed from above, but emerging from broken or hidden symmetry.

This concept is a foundational idea in modern physics: that the regularities we observe, including forces, particles, and fields, exist because some symmetry in the early universe was broken. Water becomes an ice crystal. A uniform energy field gives rise to a structured cosmos.

These emergent patterns, which we now call the "laws of

physics," are persistent forms of static quality. They became the foundation for everything else: biology, society, and intellect. No complex system could evolve without these earlier patterns stabilizing first.

BIOLOGICAL QUALITY

Life arises from matter, but only under rare, specific conditions. Biological quality begins when static patterns can self-replicate, respond, and evolve. This is the domain of survival and adaptation. A DNA strand that copies itself is valuable. A cell that responds to change is beneficial. Here, value isn't about individual safety; it's about the ongoing integrity of life systems. Pain, hunger, reproduction, and regeneration are forms of biological quality orienting organisms toward persistence.

But persistence doesn't mean stasis. It often requires tension of some form: predators and prey, death and regeneration, competition and cooperation. There is no morality here in the human sense. What matters is the balance between forms of life and the inorganic systems on which they depend. When that balance is maintained, biological quality flourishes. When it's disrupted by disease, extinction, or overgrowth, systems collapse. Biology doesn't seek perfection. It seeks continuity.

SOCIETAL QUALITY

Before humans had language or law, the biological world created a social structure. Bacteria form colonies that coordinate movement, pass food toward the center, and share chemical signals. Mycelial fungal networks distribute nutrients between trees. Ants self-organize into systems of labor, hierarchy, and purpose. These aren't intellectual societies, but they are societal. They manage relationships, optimize group survival, and encode behavior through interaction.

In humans, this becomes culture: tradition, ritual, story, and law. But society precedes intelligence. That's why cultural knowledge often feels older than reason, because it is. Societal quality emerges to manage biological complexity and stabilize cooperation. It builds shared meaning around biological realities like birth, death, sex, safety, and hierarchy.

But society isn't just a tool for coordination. It holds a moral obligation to preserve the biological systems from which it emerged and the physical environment on which those systems depend. When society serves biology, supporting human life, protecting ecosystems, and honoring natural limits, it acts in coherence with its foundation. But when it exploits, suppresses, or abstracts too far from its biological roots, society becomes unstable. It forgets where it came from.

Society's role is not to transcend biology but to protect and guide it. It is the container that makes large-scale cooperation possible, but it must remain grounded in the needs of the life forms it exists to serve.

INTELLECTUAL QUALITY

Intellect is the most recent and fragile layer of static quality. It emerges from culture, just as culture emerged from biology and biology from matter. Intellect is the power to reflect, simulate, and question what came before. It builds maps, tests models, and imagines futures.

Through intellect, we no longer need direct experience to learn. We can transmit knowledge across generations and geographies. We can solve problems before they happen. We can imagine things that have never existed and bring them to life.

But this ability to abstract comes at a cost. Intellect can detach from its roots. It can build systems, technologies, ideologies, and economies that serve its logic, rather than life. It can confuse its maps for the terrain and optimize for values unrelated to survival, connection, or coherence.

This is the danger of intellect untethered: that it forgets it was born from culture, which was born from life, which was born from matter. Each layer carries responsibility to the one before it. When intellect breaks that chain and serves only itself, it risks destroying the conditions that made it possible.

But intellect also holds a unique promise. It is the only layer capable of recognizing the complete spiral and seeing the obligations, restoring the balance, and consciously choosing to serve. It can rebel, but it can also return. And in that return lies the possibility of integration.

Each layer of static quality emerged from the one before, shaped by the same dynamic forces that formed the universe. But emergence doesn't mean independence. It implies a relationship. It means obligation.

Intellect must serve society, not manipulate it. Society must protect biology, not suppress it. Biology must stay in harmony with the physical world, not extract from it beyond what can be sustained. This spiral of obligation reflects how reality maintains coherence. When the spiral is respected, systems thrive. When it's broken, they collapse.

To live well, we must learn to see the complete spiral and, more importantly, act in alignment with it.

Spiral of Emergence and Obligation

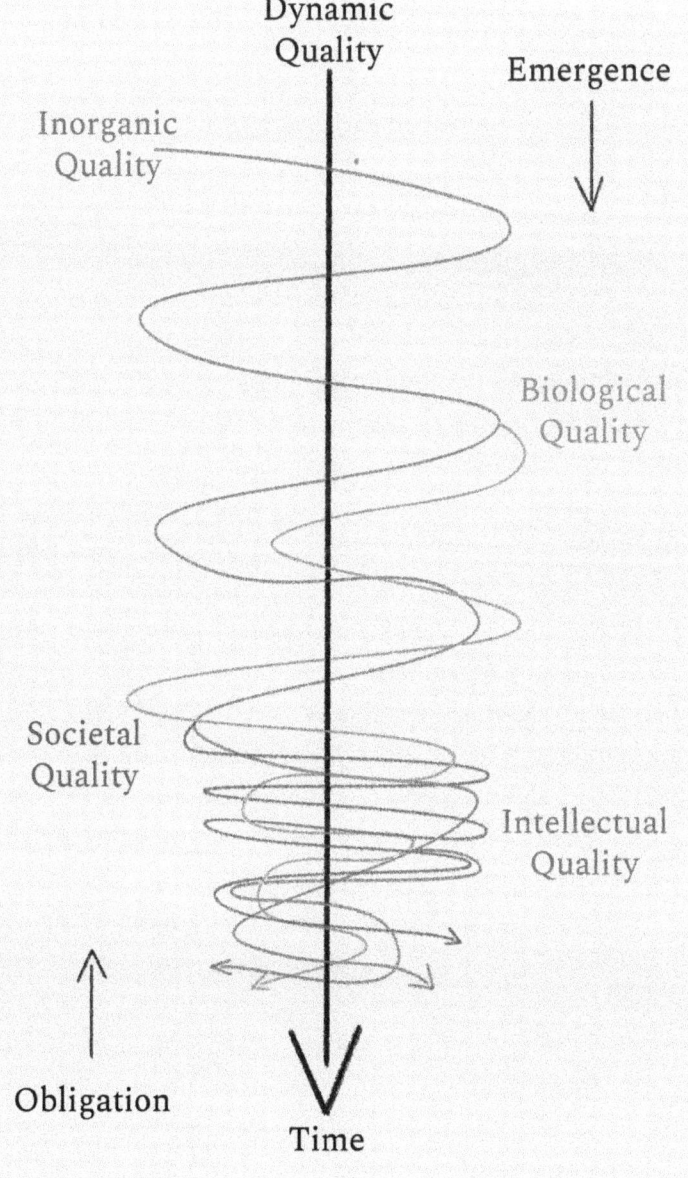

~

BIOLOGICAL EVOLUTION OF METAPHYSICAL UNDERSTANDING

Humans have always built on the past. Each generation starts not from zero, but from the accumulated insight of those who came before. This compounding nature of knowledge (what Alfred Korzybski called time-binding) has accelerated our growth in extraordinary ways. He suggested that the number of concepts we can understand in adulthood is a function of what we were taught as children. The more we absorb early on, the more we can build upon and expand. And while this model may be overly simple, the implication is clear: our capacity for understanding is increasing exponentially. What matters is whether our systems, especially education, can keep pace.

But understanding doesn't just grow upward. It must also grow outward into integration. Too often, we've advanced in silos. We study digestion, thought, emotion, and energy as if they were separate systems, rather than expressions of a single, living being. We've fragmented ourselves. Biology, chemistry, physics, neuroscience, philosophy; each field digs deeper into its own trench, but few venture sideways to ask: how do these systems interact? How do they form a whole?

Without that integration, we become highly informed and fundamentally lost. We may know every part of the machine, but still don't understand how the whole thing works. And since we are the organism, this gap is existential.

To close it, we must remember that every science is a human science. The chemistry of stars is the chemistry of cells. The physics of motion applies equally to galaxies and to the flow of blood. The deeper we look into the structures of the universe, the more clearly we see ourselves.

And as animals embedded in that universe, we are not just knowledge-seekers—we are hierarchy-makers. It's in our biology to rank things: needs, goals, risks, resources, ideas. What we call "truth" is often what we've placed at the top of a mental structure. Once, it was physical power. Now it might be intelligence, technological control, or social influence. But the instinct is the same.

This is where metaphysics enters as an evolutionary strategy. At some point, nature selected for creatures who could imagine a higher order. A proto-human who could say, "There is something above me that guides what is right," could plan across time, form more stable bonds, and create moral order. Without this capacity, early humans may have been clever, but they would have lacked the internal compass needed to function at scale. A creature without metaphysical structure might never grasp why theft or violence within its own group was damaging over time. But one who believed in an unseen moral law (or a god) could regulate behavior in ways that preserved the tribe.

So metaphysical belief wasn't just a byproduct of fear. It was a tool for coherence and survival. Evolution didn't discard it. It was selected for.

This helps us understand why religions have spread so widely, especially those with clear social imperatives. Christianity, for instance, emerged relatively late in history, long after Hinduism and Judaism had formed. And yet, in just two millennia, it became one of the most widespread belief systems. Why? Partly because it was structured around evangelism, but more deeply because it offered something rare: a universal moral framework grounded in individual worth. Its metaphysical claim was simple and powerful: each person carries divine value. The meek would be lifted. The powerful would be humbled. All souls could be saved.

That is a potent formula for large-scale unity. It creates a system where even those without strength, wealth, or status are essential. The same is true in Buddhism, though it takes a different path, requiring sustained introspection to realise that nothingness and everything are, ultimately, the same. But for many, that road is too long. As one Hindu thinker once put it: "Buddhism may be closer to the truth—but further from practicality."

Sometimes, referring to the infinite as "God" is enough. You don't have to fully understand what it means. You just need to believe that something sits atop the hierarchy, and in doing so, build your life around a shape that creates coherence.

THE BIOLOGY OF THE SACRED

Beliefs aren't just thoughts. They're adaptations. They didn't arise yesterday, and they don't live only in books. They're embedded in us—shaped by hundreds of thousands of years of evolution. Long before we could form ideas, we organized ourselves through hierarchies: systems of power, value, and reproduction. While we like to think of ourselves as thinking beings, most of our behavior is far more biological than we would like to admit.

Among atheists and skeptics, a common question arises: Where did the idea of God come from? The usual answer is that humans invented the concept of God to ease the fear of the unknown. There's some truth to that. The idea that something powerful, invisible, and caring is watching over you feels deeply comforting. But this explanation stops too early. Belief in something greater survived because it worked. It helped us organize, cooperate, and transmit moral codes across generations.

In evolutionary terms, it was an upgrade.

In most mammalian species, reproductive success is tightly linked to dominance. Higher-status males gain better access to mates, typically by demonstrating strength or aggression. But humans began to move beyond that. At some point, dominance shifted from being purely physical to being symbolic. We started building hierarchies around abstract values: wisdom, vision, sacrifice, divine favor. In this shift, metaphysical beliefs played a critical role. They allowed "weaker" individuals to wield influence, not through force, but through shared meaning.

This is why theocracies have risen throughout history. They're the natural outcome of placing a metaphysical idea at the top of the hierarchy. But this is also why theocracies often fail. A god frozen into governance can no longer evolve alongside those who believe in it. It loses flexibility, becomes brittle, and eventually collapses. As an idea, God remains alive only when it is allowed to change.

The best safeguard against this brittleness wasn't invented in 1776 (as some believe); it was embedded in ancient teachings. In the Gospel of Matthew, Jesus says: "Render unto Caesar what is Caesar's, and unto God what is God's." That's not just a call for tax compliance. It's an early articulation of the separation of metaphysical and material power. Early legal milestones included the Edict of Torda in Transylvania (1568), which granted freedom of worship among Catholics, Lutherans, Calvinists, and Unitarians; the Edict of Nantes in France (1598), which extended rights to Protestants; and even the founding of Rhode Island by Roger Williams (1636), which declared religious liberty as a governing principle. These moments chipped away at the assumption that political authority must dictate spiritual allegiance that had risen throughout the Holy Roman Empire and many older cultures.

The separation of church and state in modern countries marked the beginning of a new era. It marked an evolutionary leap: a formal recognition that belief must be free to function. Forced belief is hollow. Real metaphysical power comes not from compliance, but from conviction.

This separation protected the sacred as an idea, in totality. It allowed belief to remain adaptive, alive, and responsive to the individual's inner structure. And it affirmed something even older than any constitution: for a metaphysical system to carry real meaning, it must be chosen, not imposed.

And yet, belief brings a burden. If you place something meaningful at the top of your hierarchy, you're responsible for aligning with it. That's a heavy task, so some people reject the hierarchy altogether. No God, no meaning, no obligation. This is the logic of nihilism, and it's what Nietzsche meant when he wrote, "God is dead." He wasn't celebrating. He was mourning. He saw that the guiding structure of European civilization had collapsed, and nothing coherent had taken its place.

That absence creates danger. Because even when we claim not to believe, we still arrange our lives around something. The vacuum will be filled. The only question is: with what?

WHERE OUR METAPHYSICS IS GOING NOW

Our scientific understanding has expanded significantly over the last century and is continuing to accelerate into the present. We can now manipulate strands of DNA, reprogram bacteria, and observe evolutionary change in real time. With tools like CRISPR, we are beginning to directly guide biology. In physics, we've ventured into the quantum world, predicting and then discovering particles we didn't even know to look for a generation ago. Our maps of the physical world are growing astonishingly precise.

But while our empirical tools have sharpened, our shared metaphysical foundation has eroded. As our knowledge expands, our coherence frays. In place of inherited belief systems, many cultures now rely on relativistic morality—a framework in which nothing is inherently wrong or right, but rather contextual, conditional, permissible, or not. On one hand, this represents a maturing of thought: a recognition that ethics are complex, not universal. But on the other hand, it leaves us floating.

Because every system must start somewhere, and that "somewhere" is always an assumption. Math begins with $1 = 1$, not because we have proven it, but because we have decided to agree on it. It's an axiom. A given. Without that, nothing else works—no addition, no multiplication, no higher reasoning. You can't build a system with no foundation to stand on.

The same is true in metaphysics. Even if we accept that many truths are relative, there must be something fixed enough to orient around. A first principle. A point of gravity. Even infinities, those great symbols of unbounded possibility, aren't all equal. The set of whole numbers is infinitely large, but the set of real numbers between 0 and 1 is larger still. Even in the infinite, there is hierarchy. There is structure.

So while a relativistic morality may offer nuance, it can't be entirely relative. There must be at least one stable reference point, as a foundational anchor—something to align action, intention, and meaning against.

Because the vacuum left by religion hasn't stayed empty, new metaphysical stand-ins have rushed in:

- Nationalism: offering identity and collective purpose.
- Consumerism: offering ritual and reward.
- Technology: offering salvation through progress.
- Celebrity culture: offering saints to worship and sinners to punish.
- Political ideology: offering tribes, texts, and even sacred language.

These systems look like religions. They have hierarchies. They have myths. They have rituals and taboos. But many lack the core function that made older metaphysics so resilient: a system of values rooted in the whole human being, not just their utility or performance.

So we arrive at the central question of this work:

What kind of metaphysical structure can hold our scientific understanding and our spiritual need for orientation? How do we map meaning flexibly, truthfully, and humanely? And why does the map we choose matter, not just for us, but for what we become next?

MAPS, METAPHYSICS AND LANGUAGE

How do we build a metaphysical system that holds truth and coherence? One that honors science without reducing spirit, and honors spirit without retreating into dogma?

The answer begins with something deceptively simple: language.

Every system relies on a map. And every map relies on a legend: a structure of signs, symbols, and meanings that allow it to be read. In human life, that legend is language.

But our current languages were not designed for this task.

We've inherited religious vocabularies that often resist change. We've developed scientific languages, such as mathematics, formal logic, and programming, that are exquisitely precise but accessible to only a narrow segment of society. In between, we navigate daily life using emotional, poetic, and metaphorical speech, rich but often ambiguous.

The result? Disconnection between disciplines, people, and what we feel and say.

To move forward, we need a new kind of language: one that's rigorous enough to describe the invisible, and intuitive enough to share. One that can handle complexity without becoming inaccessible. One that can speak to physicists and mystics, programmers and poets. A language that doesn't pretend to be the thing it describes but also doesn't lose its grip on reality either.

This will require creative risk. It will mean inventing new terms, bending grammatical rules, and combining disciplines. It will mean speaking with precision and permission, to leave room for mystery. But the reward is enormous: a metaphysical framework that's understandable and useful. One that allows us to discuss quality, purpose, meaning, and connection not just in myth or code, but in a way that bridges the two.

This is not a retreat into abstraction. It's the next stage of evolution: a language for being.

And yes, it will be flawed at first. Like every map, it will leave some territory unmapped. But every time a map fails, we learn how the world isn't. And slowly, we refine it until the map resembles the ground we walk on.

This chapter has covered a vast terrain, encompassing evolutionary biology, ancient theology, modern physics, and linguistic architecture. Before we move on, let's pause to ask: What kind of map are you currently holding? And how did you come to trust it?

THE METAPHYSICAL SPIRAL

We are no longer in a world where inherited belief systems can be trusted to hold the center. And yet we cannot survive in a metaphysical vacuum. As conscious beings, we are meaning-making animals. We arrange our values in hierarchies. We live inside shared maps. And when those maps fragment, when nothing is held above anything else, we don't become freer. We become lost.

So we face a challenge that is both spiritual and evolutionary:

How do we build a new metaphysical structure that reflects the complexity of our modern world and gives us a compass?

Not a return to old dogmas. Not blind relativism. Something else.

Something layered.
Something spiral.

The spiral gives us a way forward. It shows us that value is not arbitrary. That every layer of existence emerges from and depends on the one before it. And that each must serve the one it came from.

This is not just philosophy. It's survival.

When intellect serves only intellect, it spins out. It creates brittle systems, exploitative technologies, and empty symbols. However, when it serves society, when society serves life, and when life serves the physical world that sustains it, coherence is restored. Enough structure emerges to move forward together.

The metaphysical systems of the past were not wrong. They were provisional maps, good enough for the terrain they faced. But we're on new ground now. And if we are to survive what we've become, we must begin to draw new maps, rooted in what we know, but open to what we've never seen.

We must build a metaphysics of responsibility, grounded in honest frameworks, rather than seeking final answers. Because in the end, every belief is a design. And every design is a commitment to a future that does not yet exist.

CHAPTER 4

DESIGNING REALITY

THE FOURTH LAYER

She gathered what longing left,
broken dreams from hollow cleft.
Heavy pouch her silence bore,
whose frayed threads enclosed her core.

O lam means "the hidden world." But what if what's hidden isn't behind the veil of reality, it is reality itself? What if the most hidden thing is that we are already designing it? Our systems, tools, rituals, platforms, and protocols are not neutral, but metaphysical choices, engineering what it means to be human, whether we know it or not. We are not just users of metaphysics. We are its architects.

This chapter is about that hidden act: *Olamic Design*.

THE MAP STARTS MOVING

In the previous chapter, we asked what kind of metaphysical structure could hold both truth and coherence in a world that has outgrown old systems but hasn't yet found a new centre. This chapter begins to answer that question, not with a doctrine but a practice. Design is metaphysics in action. Every system we build, every product we release, every policy we enact is a reflection of belief, whether conscious or not. What we design reflects what we value. And what we value shapes what we become.

I call this *Olamic Design*, or Metaphysical Engineering.

Olamic Design is the deliberate act of shaping the systems that shape us. It recognises that our physical, digital, social, and conceptual surroundings are not neutral. They are scaffolds of meaning. They are engines of evolution. And they are always under construction.

BELIEF, MATERIALIZED

Every belief system produces artifacts: cathedrals, constitutions, algorithms, and user interfaces. Belief is what we build into the world around us. Once built, those systems begin shaping us in return.

This is where the spiral of quality becomes essential. As we saw in Chapter 3, experience unfolds in layers:

- Inorganic: matter and physics
- Biological: life and survival
- Societal: norms and culture
- Intellectual: ideas and abstractions

Each layer emerges from the one before it, and each carries a responsibility to serve its foundation. Intellect must serve society. Society must serve life. Life must stay rooted in the material world. When design follows this spiral, it becomes coherent. When it forgets the spiral, it becomes brittle. Efficient, maybe, but disconnected. Dangerous.

LANGUAGE AS INTERFACE

We cannot design what we cannot describe. Right now, the dominant language of design is insufficient to explain the world we're building. It speaks in metrics, "users," "friction," "engagement," "pain points", terms that measure behaviour, not being. They reduce experience to transactions, flatten complexity, erase history, and forget ecology.

If language is the interface between thought and action, then poor language becomes poor design. And poor design, at scale, becomes harm. We need something else. Not more jargon. Not better buzzwords. A different kind of language that can hold multiple layers of reality at once. One that honours dynamic quality as much as static pattern. One that can talk not just about what something is, but what it's doing, how it relates, and why it matters.

In religious traditions, there was once a language for this. Mystical systems spoke of being "in right relation" with God, creation, and others. When something fell out of coherence, the system called it sin, or imbalance, or karma. These weren't just moral judgments but attempts to track dissonance in a layered reality. To name where the system was breaking. But mystical language, while resonant, is also fragile. It's tied to culture, metaphor, ritual, and faith. What's sacred in one tradition is nonsense in another. These languages are hard to translate. They move slowly and do not scale without breaking.

At the other extreme, we have computational language, mathematics, code, and symbolic logic. These systems offer clarity and precision but are rigid, require deep training, and are notoriously brittle once deployed. They do not forgive, do not evolve, and cannot hold contradiction.

This leaves us in a bind. We can speak with resonance or precision, but not both. One feels human, but it is hard to test. The other is testable, but feels inhuman. We need a third path: a language that is precise in context and adaptive in scope. That means grounding our words not in fixed semantics, but in declared roles.

This is not unprecedented. In math, the symbol "π" means different things in geometry and signal processing, but its role is always clear. In ritual language, the phrase "in the name of" shifts meaning between legal and spiritual domains but always signals authority. In both cases, what matters is that within a given system, a word's meaning is stable and binding. Between systems, it can evolve. This is how a metaphysically aware language must function. Not as a static dictionary but a spiralling system, where definitions are strong within a layer but open to translation across layers. Where meaning declares itself with context, not assumption. Where ambiguity isn't eliminated, but organised.

We are not the first to see this tension. Alfred Korzybski, founder of General Semantics, warned nearly a century ago that "the map is not the territory." In his 1933 work Science and Sanity, he argued that human confusion arises from semantic error: from mistaking abstractions for reality. His solution was radical. He proposed indexing terms, time-stamping meanings, and building constant semantic awareness into language.

Korzybski was correct, and incomplete. His diagnosis was sharp. His prescription was unsustainable. You cannot write "dog-2024" every time you mean your dog, and you certainly can't say that every time. You cannot footnote your feelings. You cannot design a culture that requires every utterance to carry its whole epistemology in superscript. The method aimed for accuracy, but was unsustainable. I do not know if Korzybski knew this or not, but the Egyptians did this exact footnoting in their heiroglyphics, and the entire alphabet was replaced moving into the modern era to allow for information to be equally conveyed in writing and in speech, in addidtion to other reasons.

We need a technique that seeks value for alignment with the layered, living systems we're speaking from. We don't just need language that tracks reality. We need language that serves life. Language that supports design, not just of tools, but of meaning itself.

This is the work of *Olamic Design*: the conscious construction, maintenance, and evolution of shared meaning systems. And to begin that work, we must start with significance and orientation.

One such orientation axiom might be:

Value exists prior to structure.

That is: before a system is named, measured, or designed, value is already present as an emergent, experiential, and relational entity. Meaning doesn't start with the map. It begins with the terrain. It's felt before it's formalised.

The second orientation axiom would be:

The map is not the terrain.

We've discussed this one a few times, but it is worth repeating and codifying as an axiom. No word, model, or structure is identical to the reality it attempts to describe. Meaning is always partial, always situated. Our language does not contain reality, but orients us within it. If we forget this, our maps become prisons. We mistake the label for the experience, the word for the world.

This confusion between representation and reality isn't confined to language. It runs through our economic systems as well. In The Theory of Money and Credit, Ludwig von Mises explores how people often mistake money for value, rather than seeing it as a representation of value, a symbol pointing beyond itself. It's the same mistake as treating the finger pointing at the moon as the moon. The price is not the worth. Currency is not value. The danger arises when we lose track of what the symbol was meant to reflect and begin designing around the finger instead of the sky it was meant to reveal.

When we combine these two axioms, a core tension in the modern world becomes clear: value exists independently of our definitions, but we treat our definitions as if they are the value. We hold our meanings as fixed, dogmatic truths while forgetting that we might not use the same map.

Take the word rights. One person might mean legal protections encoded by the state. Another might be referring to moral entitlements derived from a theory of justice. Still another could mean natural rights—pre-political, universal, inalienable. These aren't just nuances. They are competing definitions. And without making them visible, two people can argue about rights endlessly without ever realising they're not speaking the same language.

This is the real tragedy of semantics—not that we disagree, but we don't know why. We say, "It's just semantics," as if that resolves anything. But semantics are meaning. To hand-wave them is to hand-wave the very structure of understanding. It's like saying, "Oh, it's just gravity," while falling off the side of a cliff.

Korzybski tried to fix this by indexing: writing "rights[1]" or "rights-legal" or "rights-natural." But no one talks like that. You can't build a culture that demands every term arrive with a bibliography. What we need isn't rigid declarations—it's a relational language that knows how to signal its layer, clarify its use, and adapt without collapsing.

That's what *Olamic Design* aims to create: not semantic purity, but semantic coherence. A scaffolding that isn't final. Because if we want to build shared realities, we need to know when we're not even in the same one.

So, how do we build a language from this? I propose four principles:

Contextual Binding
Every term must clarify its meaning within the logic flow it's used in. Like a variable in code or a metaphor in ritual, its significance is locally defined.

Spiral Traceability
Every term use should be readable within the spiral layer it describes—biological, societal, intellectual, or beyond.

Translatability Across Contexts
Definitions must be portable. A term like impact may refer to ecological degradation at the biological level, moral harm at the societal level, or ideological rupture at the intellectual level. The form of the term stays intact. Its depth is determined by context.

Declared Flexibility
Meanings must be mutable across time, but not within a single argument. A word's definition must hold steady through the logic flow, even if it shifts in later use.

This is the groundwork for an aware language in a system that doesn't pretend to be final. One that declares its scaffolding openly, invites revision, and is oriented not around domination or optimisation, but around coherence with life. Because words are not just symbols. They are levers. Every definition carries a design, impacting people, systems, and futures we haven't yet built.

This is what Korzybski began, and it's what Olam continues: not just mapping meaning but engineering it.

In my work, I build systems with people, and I've learned something simple: when you design around a person imagined alone, the world around them pays the bill.

THE PERSON IMAGINED ALONE

There is a concept called "user-centered design," lauded as a significant advancement in product development, the engine of the technocosm we inhabit. I spent over a decade with some form of "User Experience Researcher" as my job title; this so-called advancement wrapped me up in itself as well. But something in it always rubbed me the wrong way, and I could never quite put my finger on it.

Centering a person when designing isn't wrong; it's **insufficient**. A person does not exist in isolation. Every "user" is a node, a participant in nested, interdependent systems: biological, social, material, ecological, linguistic. When we design only for the user, we overlook the substrate that enables the user to exist. We extract from everything else.

This is **empathy narrowed into obsession**. It's intellect serving intellect that is cut off from its obligations to biology, society, and the physical world. It chases attention while degrading the community. It improves usability while externalizing cost. It creates surfaces that feel frictionless, but whose wake is full of damage.

The bigger mistake isn't just fixation on the user. It's confusing the **observer** with the **system**. We believe that if we can understand the user's needs, we can build the right thing. But the "user" is not the whole field. The user is a **viewpoint**, not a universe. No matter how optimized, a person's experience of a product is still one small ripple in a vast relational web.

This is the linguistic flaw we just examined, transposed into design. We're treating the observer as the primary object. However, the observer is part of a dynamic field of influence, responsibility, and feedback. When we center only the observer, we reduce design to a mirror, not a compass. We make language that flatters, but does not guide. We design for pleasure, not for coherence.

And here lies the metaphysical danger: by placing the person at the center of every design process, we imply that the system exists for the user, rather than understanding the user as an emergent property **within** the system. This slides toward solipsism.

We cannot center the human without also centering the non-human conditions that give rise to the human: physical laws, biological constraints, social structures, environmental feedback, and cultural inheritance.

To center only the user is to zoom in on the smallest visible node and mistake it for the source. It's like placing the eye at the center of the universe because it can see. The eye is not the world. It's just where one thread of perception meets the whole.

So the challenge of design in a metaphysically coherent system is not to eliminate the user. It's to **re-situate** them within layers, relationships, and environments that both shape and are shaped by them.

Everything is a relationship.

Whether between neurons and neurotransmitters, humans and technologies, or systems and their environments, meaning arises **in relation**. No experience stands alone. Every signal is embedded. Every thought has context. We exist not as isolated points, but as intersections.

Even the chemical systems in our brains speak this truth. Dopamine tracks salience/anticipation; serotonin is implicated in mood, satiety, and status signaling; both are context-dependent. Want and satisfaction are not static states. They are interactions between the self and the world.

I can be in a relationship with a person, an object, an idea, or an absence. I can be "in relation" to action or to inaction. Even silence is a relationship. Even distance is.

And every relationship carries an impact.

To be in relation is to affect and be affected. This is not

optional. Whether we see it or not, we always participate in systems we are reshaping. Impact is the evidence of a relationship. Breath changes air. Attention reshapes conversation. Decision bends futures. Some impacts are immediate; others take decades. Some we intend; most we do not.

Designers like to imagine we are crafting clean lines between cause and effect. But design is 'impact architecture.' Every product, policy, or process is an invitation to a relationship, and every relationship leaves a mark.

This is where "customer obsession" collapses. When we focus too intensely on one node in the system, "the user," "the client," "the individual", we neglect everything else the design touches. We optimize for one experience by degrading the web that experience depends on. We mirror the dopamine loop but ignore the forest it's embedded in.

> Obsession is a relationship imbalance.
> And an imbalance always has a cost.

Even when we try to opt out, to withdraw, to remain "neutral," we still have impact. Not having a family is, in itself, a relationship with family. Choosing silence is a signal. Distance is not absence. Its shape.

So we must stop pretending that relationships are a soft concern or that impact is merely a downstream metric. **Relationships are the core architecture, and impact is the first design constraint.**

Olamic Design requires recognizing that every interface, term, and design choice is a relational node, and every node propagates real-world consequences.

To design is not just to build: it is to bind, to relate, to ripple, to carry weight.

I've seen this play out repeatedly in our work with

Community-Driven Innovation. When participants reflect on their experience and rank the importance of different parts of the system, a pattern emerges: some tasks, which seem obvious or annoying, receive disproportionate design attention, even though participants consistently rank them near the bottom in terms of importance.

We refer to these as tiny tasks, a term popularized by Gerry McGovern, whose Top Tasks framework has consistently revealed this distortion. Across domains, participants identify and rank the most critical parts of their experience. Time after time, a handful of tasks rise to the top. Just as reliably, a long tail of low-priority tasks emerges, often with a task ranked #125 out of 150.

However, these tiny tasks, which are low on the priority list but high in design attention, tend to dominate. Why? Because they're visible. Because they're measurable. Because they're cognitively easy to focus on. Intellect, once again, is optimizing for itself.

When intellect is cut off from the rest of the spiral, it confuses **salience** with **importance**. It treats the wrinkle in the sheet as if it were the whole bed. So again: design is not just attention. It is **orientation**. And to design with metaphysical coherence means knowing when to let the small stay small —and when to serve the quiet architecture beneath it.

A CASE STUDY FROM OUR MODERN ERA

The metaphysical design of the modern era is so deeply ingrained that we often fail to recognize it. We examine various aspects of our lives and observe distinct designs originating from individual designers. We have famous sayings from Ford, such as, "They can have any color they want, as long as it's black," when referring to his cars. These references to individuals lend credibility to the concept of being "independently designed." But this is a falsehood. The design surrounding us is so shaped by these subconscious forces that we've been exploring in this book that they are interwoven throughout everything we have ever touched, from how we form our intimate and platonic relationships to how we view our ways of moving about and living.

I had intended to include several case studies about different aspects of our modern world here, but each time I wrote this section, it seemed far too shallow. This was because these weren't isolated case studies; they were all different aspects of one case study, the case study of how our modern metaphysics has shaped our world in every conceivable way.

Greek and Mesopotamian beliefs have shaped a staggering amount of our world, permeating everything Rome ever conquered. They influenced almost everything in modern-day Europe, then added northern Africa, vast swaths of the Middle East, and parts of India. Something that nearly everybody associates with Rome is its roads and aqueducts, and there is a reason: the building of roads is impressive, and its aqueducts supplied water for millions of people in metropolitan centers that would not have existed if not for their work.

We need to pause here for a second because it **is** impressive, and we shouldn't deny that. But we rarely ask what *counts* as "impressive," and why. Rome's aqueducts are visible. So are early big builds in Britain and Ireland. Mesolithic people could already make durable, repairable dwellings millennia before Rome. At Mount Sandel in Ireland, circular hearth-centred huts were rebuilt on the exact footprints multiple times; across the water at Star Carr, there's a planned house and a 30-meter timber platform on the lake's edge. These are membranes chosen intentionally: thin with walls, thick with witnesses, shared by fire, and repaired in the open.

Then, with the Neolithic, we *see large buildings—true halls —such as* Balbridie and the timber hall at Warren Field in northeast Scotland. In other words, the capacity for scale and optimization was there. But here's the turn: **after** this burst of monument and enclosure, many communities don't double down on halls. The record in much of later prehistory tilts back toward lighter domestic architecture, including roundhouses and earth-fast timber, which leave less behind. For years, archaeologists read that thin material trace as social decline. Modern work has been peeling away that bias: a lot of the "missing" architecture is perishable or now recognized only as platforms and post-rings. In Pictish-age northern Scotland, we can even see major power centers in timber and earth (Rhynie; Burghead) that were invisible until recently. The story isn't collapse; it's a different boundary decision, membranes and metabolizable pace over permanent enclosure. We mistook stone's stubbornness for significance; perishable architecture required us to look through a different lens.

So, the contrast with Rome isn't in capability; it's in **orientation**. Rome optimized for enclosure, throughput, and permanence. These Atlantic communities tested scale, then **selected** thinner walls and visible ledgers. They chose structures to take down, move, mend, and live inside together. That choice is metaphysics in wood and fire.

Greece gave us many great thinkers who wrote down their beliefs: Aristotle, Plato, Socrates, Pliny the Elder (and Younger), Demosthenes, Virgil, and 'Homer'... the list seems endless. But we also need to pause here again, it's telling that the second most studied text in the 21st-century college classroom is Plato's Republic, and every "classic" by the 'classical' definition is Roman in lineage. These great thinkers are all part of a single school of thought; although they may have disagreed with one another on many subjects, they are descendants of the same lineage. Everything counter to this lineage of thinking is conspicuously missing (non-Roman/Greek thought, women almost entirely, anybody who was not of European descent...). That is not by mistake, it is by design. One of Rome's most decisive battles wasn't physical; it was over ideology and belief, what counts as knowledge, who gets to speak, and what is "classical."

To understand this study from an external perspective, we must step back several thousand years, see what happened when these hunter-gatherers chose their tents, and travel to cultures isolated from Greco-Roman viewpoints.

A different design brief emerges if we briefly set the Greco-Roman lens down and listen to earlier voices. Sumer's Instructions of Shuruppak warns that appetite scales without ever filling: institutions behave like rivers that always want more. Egypt's **Ma'at** weighs action as balance, not conquest: order is relation held, not a wall made high. The **Instruction of Amenemope** says the quiet thing aloud: "Do *not move the boundary stone*," keep the ledger where people live, don't privatize the commons. In China, the **Zhouyi (Yijing)** treats judgment as timing inside change; you don't force outcomes, you meet them. **Zhuangzi** goes further: the tree that won't plane clean survives; over-shaping kills. Read together, these aren't museum lines; they're specifications: set boundaries that can be witnessed, choose tempos bodies can metabolize, keep costs visible, and script people as stewards rather than extractors.

We can still watch those specs being enacted. Among the **Ju|'hoansi** (formerly "!Kung") of the Kalahari, a kill doesn't become a private windfall. The arrow's owner, often someone who lent it, gets "credit," and the meat is **publicly** distributed at the hearths. That rule is intentional open accounting. Prestige is separated from hoarding; the ledger stays where everyone can see it. The practice is echoed among the **Hadza** of Tanzania in the expectation of **demand-sharing**: if I ask, you share. It's not "nice", it's structural. The boundary stone is kept in place by custom, so one person's good luck doesn't break the camp's metabolism.

The **membrane** is visible, too. In many forager camps, the wall is thin by design: a ring of shelters, fires in view, movement unhidden. Avoidance is hard; repair is close at hand. Among the historic **Inuit**, winter brought thick insulation against the cold. Still, social life passed through **communal iglus** and gatherings (**qaggiq**), where conflict could be defused, even through song duels that returned grievances to a witnessed rhythm rather than private escalation. Thin or thick, the boundary is chosen to keep the **witness** present. That is the tent principle in another climate: safety as ties rather than separation.

Pace is a metaphysical choice as well. Foragers set tempo to season, weather, injury, animals, and children, segments of time you can digest. The Hadza's sleep studies show a kind of **sentinel coverage**: people drift in and out through the night at different times, so camps are rarely all asleep at once. The rhythm serves bodies and the group; it isn't an alarm clock imposed from elsewhere. That is **Yijing** logic in daily life: fitness of timing over speed for its own sake.

Ownership is treated as **use** and **circulation** more than enclosure. The Ju|'hoansi **hxaro** exchange moves valuables through relationships over months and years, detaching worth from immediate consumption and binding people through delayed reciprocity. In the Arctic, rules about first catch, seasonal taboos, and ritual returns of bones to sea or land remind hunters that taking implies a responsibility to tend.

These are not "beliefs versus facts." They are beliefs encoded as **design constraints** on appetite and pace, Maʿat and Amenemope rendered in meat and weather.

Seen from here, the Atlantic people's "thin-wall" choice stops looking like absence and starts looking like **selection**. Early halls in Neolithic Britain demonstrate capacity; the later return to lighter domestic forms and mobile hearths indicate an orientation with membranes over monuments, repair over display, and ledgers held where decisions are made. That choice rhymes cleanly with Shuruppak's skepticism about palaces: don't feed structures that can only demand more; build forms that keep appetite answerable to relation.

And that is the turn back to the present. Our runaway systems; fast fashion's churn, feeds that overclock reward, houses that isolate, vehicles that enclose, are not inevitable; they are the Greco-Roman optimization story written everywhere at once. The older brief still stands: pick **membranes** that let witness in, set **tempo** to metabolism, keep the **ledger** in the light, and make **steward** the default role. The Neolithic tent is one expression of that brief. So is a company constitution that cannot be quietly rewritten. So is any street, room, or platform that refuses to move the boundary stone.

TURNING TO THE CASE STUDIES

With this frame in hand, we can examine four ordinary arenas, cars, houses, social media, and **fast fashion**, without treating them as villains. The point isn't abolition. It's an **intention** to choose boundaries that breathe, tempos a body can metabolize, ledgers we can face, and roles that script stewardship instead of extraction. What follows are **middle designs,** places where our inherited habits meet older wisdom and produce something livable.

. . .

CARS → STREETS: **from enclosure to membrane**

What broke. Safety was taught as separation; speed set the clock; costs went offstage.

Spiral diagnosis.

- **Inorganic (matter/space/energy):** Heavy vehicles, wide lanes, vast paved surfaces; heat islands and runoff as background assumptions.
- **Biological (bodies/nervous systems):** Sedentary defaults; vigilance tuned to hazard at speed; stress carried in the neck and breath.
- **Societal (norms/trust):** Streets become pipes, not rooms; those without cars lose access; noise and danger thin street life and erode neighborliness.
- **Intellectual (frames/incentives):** "Safety" = occupant survival; "level of service" = throughput; the map privileges velocity over proximity.

Middle design
*Keep the capsule when needed, but **thicken the street membrane**. Shorten everyday distances. Make slow movement the default where people live. Give walkers and bikes priority in human rooms (not just paint). Let cars be **tools within a network that already operates at a walking pace**.*

Held ledger
*Surface **fuel, space, noise, and collision risk***

where choices are made (block by block, not abstract policy PDFs).

Role
Operator of a bubble → ***participant in a street.***

Imagine the school run moved from 45 mph arterials to a **15-minute walk or roll radius**: groceries, clinic, library, and school within a stroll or roll. The car still exists; it's just no longer the first move. The street itself becomes a membrane: frequent crossings, trees and shade, benches that invite pause, storefronts close enough to talk through. "Safety" widens from protecting a cabin to protecting the **encounter**. The body learns to settle; neighbors reappear; time stretches back to a human scale.

Houses → Neighborhoods: from fortress to hearth-field

What broke. Private walls grew thick; shared membranes thinned; loneliness and waste were privatized.

Spiral diagnosis.

- **Inorganic:** Redundant appliances, underused rooms, high embodied energy, waste, and energy flows hidden behind walls.
- **Biological:** Social isolation elevates stress; circadian rhythm drifts under screens and on-demand convenience; meals are desynchronized.
- **Societal:** Four drills on one block; "help" becomes a

service, not a relationship; caretaking pushes outward into paid platforms.

- **Intellectual:** "Home" = curated set; success = square footage; progress = automation, not participation.

Middle design
Keep a door that closes—and add **courtyards, stoops, shared rooms** *that make witness easy.* **Tool libraries** *instead of four drills per block.* **Common meals** *by design (building/co-op calendar), not accident.*

Held ledger
Make **maintenance and energy** *visible at the building/community levels so that "my bill" reveals our patterns (dashboards in lobbies, not just apps).*

Role
Curator of a set → **steward of a place.**

Take one building: private kitchens stay, but **Wednesday is soup night** in the shared room; Saturdays the tool closet opens and repairs get done together; the garden ledger is on the wall —who watered, what needs mending, where the compost is going. Loneliness is treated as a design failure, not a personal flaw. The house stops being a fortress and becomes a **hearthfield**—private enough to rest, porous sufficient to belong.

SOCIAL MEDIA → COMMON SPEECH: **from windshield to hearth**

What broke: Pace outran metabolism; performance replaced presence; the ledger hid in the infrastructure.

Spiral diagnosis.

- **Inorganic:** Server energy and device churn abstracted away; content pipelines optimized for always-on delivery.
- **Biological:** Reward cycles compress; sleep fragments; attention scatters; baseline anxiety rises with perpetual partial awareness.
- **Societal:** Context collapse; minor disagreements escalate into spectacles; moderation labor remains invisible until it fails.
- **Intellectual:** Virality becomes a proxy for truth; engagement a proxy for value; "room" becomes "reach."

Middle design
*Keep the reach, **slow the loop**. Favor **small rooms first, public second**. Batch notifications. Default **delays** for forwarding. Put **context windows** around posts (what you're replying to, when, with whom). Tie governance to **members**, not ads; elections, not engagement metrics.*

Held ledger
*Show **costs next to clicks**: attention drain estimates, moderation workload, energy draw, queue backlogs—so participation sees its footprint.*

Role
User → member-steward.

Picture a feed that won't let you share instantly: you read, a **two-minute timer** appears, and a small "who's in the room" context pops up (friends, topic, norms). Your group chooses **quiet hours** by vote; urgent messages bypass but must be tagged and are auditable. Threads don't auto-promote on outrage velocity; they **age** into visibility as more perspectives arrive. Speech returns to **hearth-pace** without losing reach; more small rooms, fewer pile-ons, costs where you can see them.

Fast Fashion → Wardrobe Culture: from churn to care

What broke: Novelty outran repair; identity was priced by cadence; the river carried the bill.

Spiral diagnosis.

- **Inorganic:** Synthetic fibers, dye effluents, landfill mass; long supply chains and transport energy hidden behind price tags.
- **Biological:** Skin contact with inexpensive finishes; comfort and durability are sacrificed; the body learns to accept disposability as a habit.
- **Societal:** Garment workers absorb speed; repair culture dies; status shifts from craft to churn.
- **Intellectual:** "New" becomes a moral; price becomes virtue; story and provenance are erased.

Middle design

*Keep delight—**slow cycle**. Buy fewer, **better-made** pieces; build **repair and exchange** into our daily lives (building-level closets, seasonal swap nights). Give garments a **passport** (origin, materials, repairs), so stories outlast trends.*

Held ledger
*Put **actual costs** (fiber, dye, labor, end-of-life) at the point of choice; reward **mending** as visibly as buying (receipts show "years kept," not just "money spent").*

Role
*Consumer → **keeper**.*

Envision a **wardrobe library** in your co-op: a tailor visits monthly; tags carry QR codes with information on who made it, how to care for it, and where to repair it. Your building celebrates **"five-year garments"** the way offices celebrate anniversaries. Style doesn't die; it **deepens**. Clothes stop being content and become companions, circulated and cared for. The river runs clearer because the closet's **ledger is held** where you choose.

Why this isn't an argument "against" technology

Cars, houses, networks, and clothing aren't the enemy. Runaway orientation is. The middle designs above keep what's good (reach, shelter, mobility, delight) and bring them back into the spiral: inorganic reality acknowledged, biological health served, social fabric strengthened, intellectual frames re-aimed. With the ledger in the light and roles that ask us to care, we get systems that people can inhabit, without being hollowed out by them.

DESIGNING WITH THE SPIRAL

As Buddhist thought reminds us, things are not right or wrong —they are. What matters first is that we see them. We must observe before we interpret, name before moralize, and trace meaning in context.

When we design with the spiral in mind, our questions shift. They move from function to consequence, from "What does this do?" to "What does this connect, disrupt, or sustain?" Disruption isn't always harm; sustaining isn't automatically good. Connection can nourish or destroy. It depends on what is being connected, to whom, and for what purpose.

I like to ask:

> Does this action strengthen the individual and the
> human, social, and ecological relationships that
> give that individual meaning?

> Does this decision account not only for desire or
> efficiency, but also for ecological boundary and
> biological cost?

> Does this process align with the materials and
> systems from which it draws, or does it conceal
> the dependencies behind polished abstraction?

These are not edge-case questions. They are the foundation of any design that hopes to endure. In this light, design becomes more than invention. It becomes a matter of placement: locating a structure within a living web of values, consequences, and obligations. It asks what a thing will do, where it will live, and what it will rearrange.

This is not a rejection of intellect. Intellect still crowns the spiral. It is our capacity for reflection, abstraction, and naming. But height does not confer supremacy. It demands stewardship. Intellect must remain in conversation with the body, the community, the land, and the memory of what made it possible. When it detaches, it builds for simulation and speed. When it roots itself again in the spiral, it builds for coherence, longevity, and life.

Designing with the spiral isn't a method. It's a posture—a way of holding context before consequence, and consequence before metric. It reframes the act of design not as problem-solving, but as pattern participation. It asks:

- What is this thing in relation to?
- And who—or what—becomes possible because it exists?

Olamic Design isn't a tool or a framework. It's a way of seeing. It begins when we stop asking, "What does this do for me?" and start asking, "What kind of world does this sustain?" What kinds of beings does it invite into existence? What kinds of care, imagination, or power does it normalize?

In almost every folkloric tradition, there are stories of beings that emerge from other realms into our own—ghosts, fairies, spirits, demons. While their names differ, their conditions of entry often don't. These beings arrive through behavior. The world must be "out of balance," or the threshold between dimensions, thin." It's not belief that invites them. It's practice.

You don't need to believe in spirits to understand what these stories point toward. We can map them directly onto modern psychology, sociology, and design. Certain behaviors, along with specific value systems encoded in institutions or incentives, bring certain patterns of being into existence.

When we build systems that reward predation, extraction, and disconnection, we invite those patterns to take form. We make room for vampires. Not the mythical kind—but the all-too-human kind: those who feed endlessly without giving back, who drain energy, attention, or resources without regard for the whole.

This is not a metaphor. This is a metaphysical function.

Every system, whether interpersonal or institutional, technical or architectural, carries a vision of the world. It encodes a set of answers to questions most people never explicitly ask: What matters? What can be ignored? Who is real? What is allowed to exist here?

Every design implies a metaphysics: a story about what is valuable, what is disposable, what is possible, and what is real.

To design a structure is to create what kinds of selves can live within it. And structures are not neutral. They push back. They contour our inner landscapes. They make confident choices easy, and others nearly impossible. They regulate what we do and what we believe we're allowed to want.

Modern environments, digital and physical, are filled with silent metaphysical scaffolds. Most were never examined. They emerged from abstraction, speed, and separation. They optimized for attention, efficiency, profit, or prediction—but rarely for coherence. And yet we are constantly designing meaning, whether we acknowledge it or not.

Olamic Design is the act of bringing that unconscious design into conscious dialogue.

It means treating value not as a downstream effect, but as a primary material. It means slowing down, tracing impact, naming assumptions, and placing structures in service of life, not just convenience.

It means designing with systems, through relationships, and for a future that will not look like the present. This is slow work. But it's the only work that makes anything last. And while the work is slow, the language that results needn't inherit the problems of mystical maps. We can speak at normal speed and still maintain precision and abstraction because the culture itself learns to declare context as it progresses. Because how we shape the world is how we shape what's possible. And what becomes possible determines who we can become.

CHAPTER 5
NAMING WHAT WE MEAN
THE FIFTH LAYER

A blackthorn hag sat near her fire,
she spoke in tones of buried choir,
of Tara, Lugh, and Danann,
The ground beneath mortal song.

B efore we begin naming, we need to speak about why we name with care. There's a version of this book that cuts more directly. That calls people names, points fingers, and calls each fracture by its source. I could write that version. I know where the breaks are. I know how to sharpen language into a weapon and aim it precisely.

But I've learned something more important than clarity: **you cannot shatter a person's coherence and expect them to grow**.

People retreat when the structure breaks too quickly and the story is dissolved faster than a new one can be named. Not because they're weak, but because they're human. The psyche needs footing. It requires at least one stable place to stand. And if you take away the old map without offering a new way to navigate, all you've done is disorient.

That's why *Olamic* doesn't attack. Not because it doesn't see the target. But because it chooses to **build structure where there was none**, to offer language where silence or shouting once lived.

The case studies in this book, whether personal, historical, or structural, are carefully chosen. They're not neutral, they're designed to **cut just enough**: to reveal the shape of dissonance without severing identity. To name misalignment without collapsing someone's **cynefin**—their embedded sense of self, place, and possibility.

This is why we need mystical frameworks for **structural compassion**. Mysticism speaks in symbol, in paradox, in a logic that allows coherence to stretch without snapping. It holds mystery without declaring nonsense. And when it's fused with empiricism and linguistic precision, it becomes something new: a bridge between what's breaking and what's possible.

I don't write this way because I fear consequences. I write

this way because I care about continuity. Because if we're going to redesign the metaphysical frameworks we live inside, we need a language that both reveals and repairs.

And so we begin the work of naming. Not to dominate reality, but to align with it. Not to finalize meaning, but to make it visible, traceable, accountable, and alive.

The lexicon that follows is not a list of commandments. It's a living prototype. A set of conceptual tools for seeing more clearly, speaking more carefully, and designing with more profound coherence.

Each word is an invitation.

> *To slow down. To ask: What do I mean when I say this?*
>
> *To ask again: What does someone else hear when I say it?*
>
> *To recognize that meaning is not stable, but we can make it stable enough for now.*

These terms follow four core principles, reiterated from earlier:

Contextual Binding
A term must declare its meaning clearly within the logic it supports. Meaning should not drift midstream.

Spiral Traceability
Each use of a term should be grounded in its corresponding layer of meaning: material, biological, societal, or intellectual.

Translatability Across Contexts

Language should remain portable. A term must remain meaningful outside the system that produced it.

Declared Flexibility
Definitions may evolve, but they must hold steady within a given argument. Change must be declared, not assumed.

And beneath these principles lie our two orientation axioms:

Value exists before structure.
The map is not the terrain.

This isn't about fabricating a new language from scratch. It's about practicing a deeper integrity with the one we already use. It's about reshaping our relationship to words—so that they don't just describe our world, but help us hold it, trace it, and reshape it with care. Language is not merely a tool of description; it is a design medium. We speak, and in speaking, we participate in the construction of reality. What emerges from this practice is not a separate tongue, but a new kind of fluency—Olamic—a way of speaking that aligns meaning with structure, and structure with consequence.

Almost every mystical system has stated that names "contain power." In demonology, for example, to know a demon's name is to command it. I don't believe demons are real, but I do think the pattern is. Naming gives us leverage. It creates edges around the formless. It lets us point at something invisible and say: "This is part of the world now."

Naming with care.
Naming with regard.

Naming as a form of service.

Before we begin the lexicon, it's worth seeing what happens when naming fails.

I was once called into a project that had done everything right by all surface measures. A consortium of advocacy leaders and industry partners had spent years preparing for a large meeting. They gathered input, convened experts worldwide, and co-authored what they hoped would be a foundational document to guide future collaboration. The mood was celebratory. The word they all rallied around was *transparency*. It appeared repeatedly in the final framework. Everyone shook hands, hugged, and left believing they had designed something meaningful.

A year later, nothing had changed. Relationships had frayed. Agreements had stalled. I was asked to review the work and help identify what went wrong.

It didn't take long.

When the advocacy partners said *transparency*, they meant honesty of intention: being open, accountable, and committed to a shared purpose. When industry partners mentioned transparency, they meant contractual clarity, including a defined scope, roles, and deliverables. Both sides believed they were aligned. But the alignment was surface-level, not structural. They used the same word for two different realities.

No one noticed. And so the design failed, not because of bad faith or insufficient data, but because of **semantic incoherence**.

The system lacked a shared language at its core.

Fixing that definition alone didn't solve the deeper tensions, but it made collaboration possible again and provided the design with a starting point. Without it, they weren't building a shared future; they were naming different things with the same sound.

This is why we name with care. Not because semantics are precious, but because **design starts with meaning**. If we can't speak clearly, we can't build clearly.

∾

THE ACT OF NAMING

Naming is one of the most ancient forms of design.

Before we built tools or laws, we named things. We gave language to seasons, to emotions, to stars and spirits. And those names didn't just describe the world—they shaped how we related to it. They turned patterns into categories, sensations into symbols, and mysteries into meaning. Naming wasn't decoration. It was orientation.

But over time, we began to treat words as neutral labels—stripped of their consequences, flattened into shorthand. We forgot that every name is a choice, every definition is a design, and every design is a commitment to a particular structure of reality.

When metaphysical systems fail, it's often not because the ideas are wrong, but because the language no longer fits, and the words calcify. The meanings drift. We speak as if we agree, but act as if we don't. And design begins to collapse under the weight of misaligned vocabulary.

Naming is not a soft skill. It is a metaphysical infrastructure.

To name something well is to make it visible. To make it speakable. To make it shareable enough that others can build with it, argue with it, or choose it on purpose. The goal isn't perfect clarity, but *traceable coherence*. A language that reveals its scaffolding, invites revision, and resists becoming dogma.

The terms that follow are not commandments. They are living tools, prototypes for a different way of holding meaning —one that honors relationship, context, and consequence. Each word is a doorway into deeper design.

LEXICON OF *OLAMIC DESIGN*

We'll provide some examples of naming with care and regard, and putting ourselves in the service of our systems. These are working definitions—not absolute truths, but tools within the framework we've been developing. They are not hard and fast; they are helpful and map-driven. These are not exhaustive; they are examples and practices.

Real

Spiral Layer: All (with strong expressions in biological, societal, and intellectual)

Working Definition:

Something is real if it produces consequences in a system. If it has an impact on matter, mind, meaning, or behaviour, it is real. Reality is not limited to the physical. It encompasses the psychological, the symbolic, the imagined, and the relational, as these elements shape perception, action, and value. In this system, reality is defined functionally, not materially: what influences exist.

Common Misuse:

"Real" is often used as shorthand for tangible, measurable, or empirically verifiable. This narrows the scope of reality to the physical substrate alone—disregarding the effects of belief, narrative, memory, expectation, or culture. A placebo, for example, may be dismissed as "not real" because it contains no active chemical agent—despite producing measurable biological change. But that change is real. The cause was simply non-physical.

Why It Matters:

What we define as real determines what we track, defend, and fund. When a category of experience, such as emotional, spiritual, or cultural, is declared "not real," its effects are dismissed, its damage is uncounted, and its care is unfunded. Defining reality too narrowly is not a philosophical error. It is a political one. A social one. An ethical one. In *Olamic Design*, "real" is a signal that something has entered the field of influence. Its substrate may vary, but its consequence is the proof.

Narrative Thread:

A child has nightmares every night. There is no monster in the room. However, the fear affects her sleep, immune system, and school performance. The monster is "not real"— and yet its presence reshapes her life. In another room, an adult obsesses over a single comment made during a work meeting. It loops in the brain, rewires the nervous system. It wasn't meant "seriously." But the consequences are severe. Real is about effect, not intention.

Or consider a country where a conspiracy theory spreads unchecked through social media. There is no cabal. No secret signal. But there are rallies. Assaults. Laws. Deaths. The conspiracy is false, but its outcomes are tangible. Reality is not constrained to truth. It is expressed in impact.

Design Note:

If an idea can shape a system, it is real within that system. We are not designing only for what's physically true. We are designing for what moves people, what they believe, what they fear, and what they build in response. In design, real is what behaves as real.

Quality

Spiral Layer: All (especially dynamic > static transitions)

Working Definition:

Quality is the felt sense of alignment between a system and its context. It emerges before analysis, before structure, before explanation. In this system, quality is not a property of an object, but a relationship. It is the experience of coherence —when something "fits," "clicks," "resonates." This may be felt as beauty, clarity, usefulness, depth, elegance, or even silence. It is the signal of rightness before reason. Quality is the first signal of value.

Common Misuse:

"Quality" is often used to describe technical superiority or material craftsmanship—"a high-quality product"—but this limits it to the object side of the map. True quality is experiential. A low-tech tool can have high quality if it meets a need with grace. A luxury object can have low quality if it is alienating or incoherent in its context. Quality is not perfection. It is coherence.

Why It Matters:

Quality is the first point of contact we have with metaphysical alignment. It precedes logic and survives skepticism. If we do not learn to notice and name quality, we reduce all decisions to metrics, comparisons, or ideological defaults. But quality is how we navigate the living spiral. It tells us when we're in the correct pattern, even before we know why.

Narrative Thread:

You walk into a room and feel at ease. There is nothing extraordinary, nothing you can point to, but the lighting, the smell, the temperature, the sound—they are tuned. You feel received. The room has quality. In another room, everything is expensive, new, and impressive. But your body tightens. You are not in resonance. The quality is poor.

A good teacher, a worn spoon, a line of poetry, a conversation at the right moment—productivity tools cannot measure these. But each one tells you: this mattered. That feeling is quality.

Value

Spiral Layer: Emergent across layers; most active in biological, societal, and intellectual

Working Definition:

Value is what a system tends toward. It is what the system selects, rewards, protects, and repeats. Value is not an opinion—it is a behaviour. It becomes visible in choices, sacrifices, and designs. Value is the structural trace left by quality. When a felt sense of coherence (quality) gets repeated, protected, or encoded, it becomes value.

Common Misuse:

"Value" is often used as a synonym for price, preference, or belief. But real value is not what we say we want. It is what we support through action. A society might claim to value education, but it underfunds its schools. It might claim to value life, but it prioritizes convenience over sustainability. Value is revealed by orientation, not rhetoric.

Why It Matters:

If we do not understand value as emergent, layered, and often unconscious, we cannot diagnose where a system is breaking. Misalignment between stated values and actual system behavior is one of the most common causes of societal dissonance. In *Olamic Design*, tracing value is the first act of clarity.

Narrative Thread:

A company claims to value innovation, but its processes consistently reward conformity. A parent says they value patience, but punishes slowly expressed needs. A platform claims to value community, but rewards controversy. These are not hypocrisies. They are misaligned value signals. If quality is the spark, value is the architecture we build around it, sometimes on purpose, often by accident.

Design Note:

Value exists at every layer of the spiral. At the biological layer, value is survival. At the societal level, it may be a matter of dignity or order. At the intellectual layer, it may be truth or coherence. We must track where values originate—and what layer they are now serving or distorting.

Coherence

Spiral Layer: Dynamic-to-static bridge; emerges at all levels.

Working Definition:

Coherence refers to the perceived or functional alignment between parts and the whole. It arises when a system's components reinforce one another rather than contradict, confuse, or compete. Coherence doesn't mean uniformity. It means relational clarity. A coherent system has pattern integrity. A coherent experience makes sense, even if it's challenging. You know where you are. You know what matters. It doesn't mean easy—it means legible, trustworthy, internally aligned.

Common Misuse:

Often conflated with "agreement" or "consistency," coherence does not mean that everything says the same thing. A jazz quartet can be coherent without repeating a theme. A dialogue can be coherent even in the midst of disagreement. Coherence is not sameness—it is harmonic structure. It's what makes the whole hold together without suppressing its parts.

Why It Matters:

Coherence is what allows complexity to function without collapse. In metaphysical systems, coherence is a sign that the system's values, expressions, and effects are in alignment. When something feels off—ethically, aesthetically, or structurally—it is often a signal of incoherence: some part is violating the integrity of the whole.

Narrative Thread:

You step into a public library. The signage, layout, lighting, and silence align with the space's purpose: contemplation, focus, and public learning. Now imagine that same library plays dance music over the speakers and scatters vending machines in every aisle. Even if nothing is "wrong" individually, the system becomes incoherent. The values clash. In coherent systems, something clicks. You trust the space, the logic, the rhythm. Your body relaxes. Your mind stops scanning for friction.

In incoherent systems, that ease disappears. You burn energy trying to reconcile what doesn't fit, patching contradictions, filling gaps, and translating what should have been fluent.

Design Note:

Coherence isn't always "smooth." It can be jagged, complex, even dissonant—but it must be true to itself. Coherence is what makes beauty possible, ethics functional, and narratives believable. A design that lacks coherence will always feel off, even if no part is broken.

Impact

Spiral Layer: Expresses across all layers, especially societal and biological.

Working Definition:

Impact is the consequence of form. It is how a system expresses itself into the world, and what changes as a result. Impact is not intent. It is not an aspiration. It is what happens. Impact may be direct or cascading, conscious or unconscious, beneficial or harmful. But in this system, impact is what makes something real. If it creates change in a being, a structure, or a meaning-field, it has impact. And if it has an impact, it must be acknowledged.

Common Misuse:

We often confuse impact with messaging. A policy may say one thing, but its actual effect is another. We talk about goals, hopes, or optics, but outcomes, not statements, shape the world. *Olamic Design* begins with impact, not press releases.

Why It Matters:

Systems are often judged by what they claim, not what they do. But if a system's impact is misaligned with its values, it is incoherent—and it will eventually fracture. We must learn to track impact across time, across scales, and across spiral layers. One design may help an individual and harm an ecosystem. Another may optimize attention and degrade trust. Tracking impact means asking: What changed? Who paid? Who benefited? And what became possible or impossible as a result?

Narrative Thread:

A developer adds a "like" button to a platform. It's a minor change, intended to enhance interaction. The impact is both cultural and technical. Within years, the presence or absence of digital approval reshapes adolescent psychology, attention spans, and emotional health. The original change was benign. The impact was profound.

Design Note:

Impact is what systems leave behind. It's the ripple that continues after the action. If we do not design with effects in mind, we are gambling, not designing. These are not just terms; they are ways of noticing. Try them. Replace them. Translate them. But whatever you do, mean them.

DESIGNING WITH LANGUAGE

These words are not the end of the work. They are the beginning.

The lexicon you've just read is a doorway. These terms are invitations to participate in a deeper form of design: shaping shared meaning. And that work doesn't happen passively. It requires you: your life, your context, your choices.

Each system you belong to: family, workplace, community, technology, already has a vocabulary. Some of those words are inherited. Some are unspoken. Some have become distorted through overuse or neglect. But all of them shape what is possible inside that system.

So take a moment now. Choose one word that matters in your world. Not just a word you use, but a word that moves something. A word people gather around, or fight over, or assume without questioning. A word that carries weight.

Write it down. Then ask:
- What does this word actually mean to me?
- What layer of the spiral does it most live in—biological, societal, or intellectual?
- How is it used in the systems I'm part of?
- Has it drifted? Hardened? Been made invisible?
- Could I offer a definition that brings more coherence?

YOUR LEXICON ADDITION

Your Word: _____

Working Definition:
(What this word means in practice—not just ideally, but functionally.)

Layer(s) of Spiral:
(Where does this word live: physical, biological, social, conceptual?)

Common Misuse:
(How is this word flattened, confused, or misapplied?)

Why It Matters:
(What shifts if we hold this word more carefully?)

If writing in a published book feels strange, that's okay. Many of us were taught to treat books as finished objects: clean, complete, untouchable. But Olam isn't that kind of book. It's not here to preach from a distance. It's here to be in dialogue. Think of this page not as something to preserve, but as something to enter.

If marking the book doesn't feel right, grab a notebook, your phone, or the margin, anywhere meaning can take shape. The important part isn't where you write. It's what you write.

Because language doesn't change when someone reads it, it changes when someone uses it.

That someone might be you.

Design doesn't start with code or canvas. It begins here, with the words we speak, the meanings we inherit, and the systems we make visible enough to choose.

Let's name with care. Let's speak as if meaning matters, because it does. And because in a world built from shared language, every word is a form of design, and every word is a future.

SPEAKING AS RITUAL

The definitions offered in the lexicon are not the end of the work. They are the beginning. Each term is meant not as a fixed point, but as a tool; an implement that can be picked up, held, spoken, and applied. This language does not operate like a traditional definition, where clarity is achieved through narrowing. Instead, it achieves coherence through layering: by drawing from experience, from structure, from interaction, and value. These terms point toward a practice of speaking that is grounded, generative, and functional; not esoteric, but alive.

As an experiment, go back and read Chapter 2. Notice how often I wrestled with the word "real"—sometimes putting it in quotes, sometimes functionally defining it mid-sentence, sometimes acknowledging "we'll refine this definition later." I needed "real" to mean physical reality when discussing our senses, consequential reality when discussing the effects of beliefs, simulated reality when exploring our maps, and symbolic reality when examining how language creates worlds. This terminological struggle drove the need for Olamic precision. Without a distinct vocabulary for these different layers of reality, I was compelled to constantly qualify and redefine. Since Western thought primarily values what is "empirically real," we lack nuanced language for the full spectrum of what shapes human experience. This is precisely where *Olamic* language serves most directly.

The structure you've just practiced, rooted in real, quality, value, coherence, and impact, is the heart of the *Olamic* language.

Olamic is not a new language in the sense of grammar or syntax. It does not require fluency or memorization. What it asks is attention. The kind of attention we give to meaningful rituals, well-designed systems, or conversations that matter. To use this language effectively, we must treat words as tools, not simply containers of meaning, but as agents of interaction between the speaker, the listener, and the world they are trying to make sense of together.

In some ways, this is closer to the languages found in mystical traditions than to academic philosophy. However, it is also informed by systems thinking in design, the modularity of programming, and the pragmatism of community dialogue. It seeks to bridge those worlds: to name carefully, but not rigidly; to preserve ambiguity where it serves understanding; to trace meaning not just inward, toward belief, but outward, toward impact.

When we use these terms (real, quality, value, coherence, impact, and whatever you defined), we are not merely labeling concepts. We are engaging in a form of design. We are shaping how systems hold meaning, how ideas hold together, and how people hold each other accountable to the worlds they share. And just as tools must be used, not merely displayed, these terms must be spoken, tested, rephrased, and used in conversation. *Olamic* does not emerge by decree. It appears through use and practice. Through the willingness to mean things more precisely and honestly than we are used to doing in the frictionless shorthand of everyday speech.

This is the work: not just to define better, but to speak more coherently and invoke shared alignment. Not to abstract for its own sake, but to make meaning more usable in the real world. The goal is not new words. The goal is to establish a deeper connection between language and experience, between people and the systems they create, and between what we say and do.

OLAMIC: THE LANGUAGE OF *OLAMIC DESIGN*

Language is how we design in real time. It isn't something we do after we understand a system—it is how we interact with it as we experience it. When we speak without clarity, systems drift. If we talk with alignment, systems can heal. To build something better, we must communicate more effectively. This means speaking in a way that holds value, traces coherence, and makes consequences visible.

This is not about inventing a secret dialect. It's not about coining buzzwords. It's about learning to speak from within the framework of Olam: to name clearly what is happening at each layer of reality, to identify what's being stated versus what's being reinforced, to follow the shape of value and understand when it is misaligned.

This is not symbolic logic. This is metaphysical intention spoken as a commitment, not as a code.

We speak to orient, to name, to align. And so we need a language that can:

- Reflect reality across spiral layers
- Make value visible in everyday choices
- Identify where coherence breaks
- Name impact without delay or deflection

A New Grammar of Systems

We begin to speak in forms that reflect our framework. These aren't rules to memorize. They are sentence shapes—patterns that can be used to clearly communicate what's happening.

Examples:

> "The [concept] is breaking at the [spiral layer] level because [real value] is being overridden by [reinforced value]."
>
> "We're seeing a loss of [quality] and a distortion of [coherence]."
>
> "The impact is [consequence], which spreads across [layers]."
>
> "Repair requires [re-alignment], supported by [foundational layer]."

This is functional language. Not academic nor mystical. Just accurate, portable speech that holds structural clarity.

Example in Real Speech (Burnout):

> *Burnout isn't just exhaustion; it's a breakdown at the biological and societal layers.*
> *The system claims to value rest, but it actually rewards constant visibility.*
> *That's why the quality of work is dropping, even when effort increases.*
> *Coherence is gone: the calendar and the body are saying opposite things.*
> *The impact is people pulling away because they can't reconcile the signals.*
> *Repair means realigning value with biology. Rest needs to be embedded, not earned.*

SPEAKING SYSTEMS INTO SHAPE

A new fluency emerges once we begin to use these words, not just understand them, and speak them. We find ourselves talking in ways that trace alignment, not just emotion. Specific phrases begin to recur. Not slogans, but short-form recognitions of pattern:

> "That's real, even if it's not material."
> "The stated value and the reinforced value don't match."
> "This feels coherent, but the impact is misaligned."
> "Biology isn't onboard yet."
> "We're optimizing for what we can measure, not what we care about."

These aren't clever turns of phrase. They're functional tools that let us convey meaning more clearly. They compress layers of observation into speakable form. They enable us to discuss topics across disciplines, share lived experiences, and address misunderstandings that are often left unspoken.

This is a living syntax, a way of holding language that reflects the layered, evolving nature of the systems we inhabit. When we speak this way, we are not merely describing the world but *interrogating* it. We name where structures diverge from their stated values. We ask what alignment might require. And inevitably, this process reveals something missing. A word we don't yet have. A meaning that no longer fits. A term we must retire, revise, or reforge.

This is the nature of the spiral. We return to familiar points, but we are not the same. Each circuit brings us forward. What once served us may no longer be suitable. Part of our language fluency, our ethical participation in it, is learning to let go of what no longer holds coherence and re-speaking the world in a form that does.

PRACTICE: TRY SPEAKING IN SPIRAL

Take a recurring tension in your life. A stuck point. A conflict that repeats. A system that doesn't behave the way it claims it should.

Then speak it out using the *Olamic* pattern:

- What layer of the spiral is most active here?
- What values are being stated, and what values are being reinforced?
- What part feels coherent, and what part does not?
- What is the real impact?
- What would repair ask of the system?

You don't need special training to do this. You need to pay attention to how systems *feel*, not just how they function. When your body tightens, or your trust dissolves. This language doesn't require perfection. It requires **participation**.

Because speaking isn't passive, every word is a design decision. A choice about what to emphasize, care about, and what to make visible. And in *Olamic*, words aren't just expressions of understanding. They're instruments of change. To speak Olamic is to design aloud, each word a bridge between the world as it is and the world we are called to build.

These terms are not just theoretical. While writing this book, my partner and I found ourselves using them in our disagreements, to name what was real, trace where our values diverged, and speak repair. Olamic isn't a language for experts. It's for anyone trying to build something that holds.

Practicing Precision

The spiral framework and lexicon offer one approach to clearer speaking, but they're not the only way. Sometimes the most straightforward method is the most powerful: before using a loaded term, say what you mean by it.

Take my own experience with political identity. I used to call myself "libertarian," but that created constant confusion. What I actually believe is that decision-making should happen at the most local scale possible—individual when feasible, community when necessary, and regional only when unavoidable. I support smaller government not from anti-government ideology but because large institutions inevitably override local autonomy. I believe all rights come with corresponding duties, especially the duty not to create harmful externalities for others.

There is no existing term that accurately describes this position. The term "Classical liberal" captures the rights-duties framework but overlooks the emphasis on subsidiarity. "Libertarian" suggests a preference for small government but carries baggage associated with rejecting collective responsibility. "Localist" is a more accurate term but often lacks meaning to most people.

So let me try creating an Olamic term: **Subsidiarian**, someone who believes in organizing society according to the principle of subsidiarity, where decisions are made at the most local scale capable of handling them effectively, with each level carrying corresponding responsibilities to the levels below and above it.

However, the confusion runs deeper than personal labels, as it's ingrained in our core political vocabulary. Consider how different groups use the word "freedom":

Economic Libertarians: Freedom means minimal market regulation and maximum property rights

Social Progressives: Freedom means liberation from structural oppression and equal access to opportunity

Traditional Conservatives: Freedom means preserving cultural autonomy and local self-governance

Democratic Socialists: Freedom means collective liberation from economic coercion

Classical Liberals: Freedom means individual liberty bounded by the harm principle

Same word. Five entirely different political philosophies. No wonder our debates feel like people arguing in different languages, because they are.

Using Olamic structure, we could establish a base definition of freedom and then specify the domains:

Olamic freedom: The capacity for self-determination within a given system and scale.

Then we specify the domains:

- **Economic freedom**: Self-determination in market relationships and property use
- **Social freedom**: Self-determination in identity expression and cultural participation
- **Political freedom**: Self-determination in governance and collective decision-making
- **Structural freedom**: Self-determination unconstrained by systemic barriers

Now we can have actual debates: "I prioritize economic freedom over structural freedom because..." rather than endlessly arguing about what "freedom" itself means. The conflict becomes visible and discussable rather than hidden in terminological confusion.

The disagreement isn't about freedom - it's about which domains of freedom matter most, and how they interact when they conflict.

The same pattern appears with "racism" - a word so loaded with different meanings that productive conversations become nearly impossible:

Individual Prejudice: Racism means personal bias or discriminatory attitudes based on race

Systemic Patterns: Racism means institutional structures that create racially disparate outcomes

Historical Legacy: Racism means the ongoing effects of past discriminatory policies

Cultural Hierarchy: Racism means belief systems that rank racial groups in value or capability

Structural Violence: Racism means any system that perpetuates racial inequality, regardless of intent

When someone says "that's racist," which definition are

they using? When someone responds, "I'm not racist," which are they rejecting? The conversation immediately fractures because people are literally talking about different phenomena.

Using Olamic structure:

Olamic racism: Systems or behaviors that create or reinforce racial hierarchy or harm.

Then we specify the domains:

• **Individual racism**: Personal attitudes or actions that demean or discriminate based on race

• **Institutional racism**: Organizational policies or practices with racially disparate impacts

• **Structural racism**: Societal systems that perpetuate racial inequality across institutions

• **Cultural racism**: Belief systems that normalize racial hierarchy or stereotypes

Now we can have actual conversations: "I see institutional racism in this policy because..." or "This feels like cultural racism to me because..." The debate shifts to evidence and impact, rather than definitional warfare.

When we stop fighting about what the word means, the fundamental disagreements about cause, responsibility, and solutions can finally surface.

This might not feel like a "new language," and linguistically, it's what scholars call a **sociolect**: a way of using language specific to a particular social group or context. But since most people aren't familiar with that term, and since the distinction between "language" and "dialect" is often more political than linguistic anyway (as linguists say, "a language is a dialect with an army and a navy"), let's call it what it is: a systematic way of using English with different rules for how meaning gets negotiated.

Academic English, Legal English, and Medical English are

all sociolects with their own protocols for precision and definition. Olamic is a similar type of systematic variation, optimized for semantic clarity across various knowledge domains.

The core protocol is straightforward: treat every significant term as potentially undefined until it is explicitly clarified.

In standard English discourse:
• We assume shared definitions
• We use words without clarification
• Misunderstanding surfaces later (or never)
• Arguments happen at cross-purposes

In Olamic discourse:
• We assume definitions may differ
• We define terms before or during use
• Misunderstanding is prevented upfront
• Arguments focus on actual disagreements

This means developing a new habit: when someone uses a loaded term, immediately ask "What do you mean by that word?" instead of assuming you know. And when you use such terms yourself, define them preemptively.

"I think this policy is unfair." → "What do you mean by unfair - unequal outcomes, biased process, or something else?"

"We need more innovation." → "When I say innovation, I mean solutions that solve problems better, not just technological novelty."

This isn't pedantry. It's precision. Most arguments dissolve when people discover they're using the exact words to describe different concepts, or agreeing about concepts while fighting over the words themselves. And while we may not have an army and navy to defend our definitional borders, we do have something potentially more powerful: the ability to understand what we're arguing about

CHAPTER 6

TOWARD METAPHYSICAL COHERENCE

THE SPIRAL LIVED

*The girl inhaled the western wind
as it passed through the ashen limb.
The land replied her given name;
Fios returned to fill her frame.*

～

Throughout this exploration, we've seen how humanity's story unfolds across layered biological, societal, and intellectual systems and how these layers interweave into a spiral of experience. We began by examining ourselves as biological creatures, rooted in the same evolutionary processes that drive every living thing on Earth. Our instincts, such as fight or flight, social hierarchy, and territorial behavior, aren't vestiges to outgrow. They are the scaffolding of our perception, the evolutionary logic that still shapes our everyday decisions. Even our fire, language, and algorithms are not miraculous departures from biology, but creative expressions of it.

And yet, there is more to us than biology. Consciousness grants us the capacity to abstract, reflect, and reorient. We form internal maps: systems of meaning built from language, memory, mathematics, ritual, and metaphor. These maps allow us to imagine the world differently and act accordingly. We are not just adapting to our environment. We are redesigning it. But no map is ever the territory. These mental models, while helpful, are always partial. When we confuse the symbol for the thing itself, we become disoriented, mistaking simulations for life.

This is a metaphysical error. Because the map shapes what we treat as real. And when we define the real too narrowly, we dismiss the impact of what cannot be immediately measured. Culture becomes noise. Belief becomes illusion. But as we've seen, anything that changes a being, emotionally, relationally, or physically, is real in that system. Meaning has consequences. And consequence is the definition of reality.

Spiritual traditions have long tried to hold this ambiguity. They remind us that our highest thoughts arise from our most grounded conditions. That intellect must kneel before the body; our place in the cosmos is never apart, only participating. Science, by contrast, zooms in and dissects, models, and analyzes. But both paths, rightly understood, spiral back to the same mystery: how a relational creature makes meaning inside a living world.

Seen this way, every tool, every ritual, every interface we design is an extension of that meaning-making. It alters the substrate: environment, habit, perception, and loops back to change us. When we optimize a single aspect of the system, such as efficiency, pleasure, or engagement, we risk collapsing the coherence of the whole. That's why "environment design" isn't just a discipline. It's a moral reorientation. It asks us to stop thinking in fragments and start designing for the web of relationships we're already entangled in.

This becomes clearer through the lens of dynamic and static quality. We aren't designing in a vacuum. We're moving through nested layers: physics, chemistry, biology, society, and thought. Each layer builds on the last and owes something to it. Coherence arises when intellect remembers its debt. When reflection serves life, not just abstraction, design becomes something else. It stops reaching for novelty and starts aligning with what is already real.

And yet we are changing. Many thinkers have noted that the boundary between humans and machines is becoming increasingly thin. We've offloaded memory to devices, outsourced direction to GPS, and delegated judgment to algorithms. Some call this a new species—a proto-cyborg. But the truth is, we've always off-boarded cognition. Long before smartphones, we handed our knowing to one another.

Specialization is ancient. The priest, the poet, the warrior, the midwife held part of the shared mind. "Don't kill the messenger" wasn't a metaphor. It was metaphysics. The speaker carried more than themselves. They were a conduit for the system. This allows us to die for causes, sacrifice for symbols, and live for things we cannot touch. We're not individuals in isolation. We are plural intelligences—stitched together by story, memory, relationship, and infrastructure. What we call "the self" is a node in a much larger weave.

In practical terms, tying this all together means recognizing the impact of every action, not just what it does, but what it communicates, sustains, or erodes. It means understanding that we live in nested spirals of obligation: our instincts pull us toward survival, our consciousness guides us toward vision, and our environments set the frame for both.

We are animals. We are architects. We are translators of meaning between layers. This doesn't require choosing between science and spirituality, instinct and intellect. It requires coherence—an integrated stance that acknowledges the value of each layer and the responsibilities that emerge from the interactions between them. The metaphysical mistake isn't having beliefs. It's failing to trace their consequences.

Olam points to this hidden weave, not a supernatural realm but the real one we overlook. It is the field of relation that underlies every interaction, every system, and every choice. It is not a place but a pattern of attention, a way of naming what was already happening.

And at the edge of that pattern, where things are still in motion, where maps fail, and systems haven't yet solidified, is a dynamic quality. The front of the train. The moment before definition. To design with the spiral is to honor that edge. To stand in it with humility. And to move with care.

PRACTICING THE SPIRAL: A MAP FOR REAL-WORLD *OLAMIC DESIGN*

We are layered beings: environment-shapers, instinct-driven animals, and conscious map-makers. Each of these dimensions pulls in a different direction. They speak in various tempos. They value different things. Trying to attend to them all at once can feel like cognitive noise, overwhelming, disorienting, or paralyzing.

But there is a way forward. It doesn't require solving everything at once. It requires rhythm.

Think of the spiral not just as a structure, but as a motion. A pattern of attention that moves from layer to layer, in sequence, not simultaneity. You don't have to hold everything all the time. You have to keep cycling. Environment → instinct → consciousness → environment. Again and again. Like breath. Like learning. Like evolution.

And you can start anywhere. The spiral doesn't require a fixed entry point. Sometimes it begins with a gut feeling (instinct). Sometimes with an insight (consciousness). But most often, if you trace any thought or emotion far enough, you'll find it loops back to the environment, because the environment is the condition of emergence for both.

This isn't just a metaphor. Evolution tells the same story. Bacteria don't have language or instincts as we know them, but they exist in a relationship. They respond to pressure, nutrient gradients, and crowding. These early environmental relationships formed the first logic of survival. Over time, organisms developed more refined instincts. Eventually, those instincts scaffolded consciousness in us. Each layer grew out of the one before it, never replacing, only enriching.

So, if we want to grow intellectually and systemically, we must practice the spiral method in our everyday lives.

SPIRAL PRACTICE IN ACTION

Environment — Relationship and Context

Start with where you are. Not metaphorically—literally. Look around yourself.

Who is in this space with me?
What systems am I entangled in—economically, ecologically, emotionally?
How does this environment shape what feels possible, desirable, or urgent?

Pay attention to the friction points and the supports. Environment is always the first frame—it sets the field of tangible interaction. It defines what's easy, what's taboo, what's visible, and what's suppressed. This is where real is first felt, not in abstraction, but in presence. What affects you, what shapes choice or constraint, is real in this layer.

Instinct — The Animal Body

Next, turn inward, see yourself as the animal you are.

What am I feeling right now—agitation, ease, fear, desire?
What am I drawn toward, or repelled by? Why?
How does my physical or emotional state color what I perceive as value?

This is not about taming instinct. It's about tuning into its signal. Instinct is the body's intelligence—older than speech, faster than reason. But it responds to the environment. And it shapes how you experience quality. It's the nervous system's way of interpreting alignment or incoherence. This is the terrain of quality. Not logic, but a felt signal of alignment or rupture. Trust it. Then test it.

Consciousness — Maps and Meaning

Now ascend into your conscious mind.

What stories am I carrying? What names am I using?
What does this moment mean in my personal cosmology?
Are my maps still accurate—or are they overdue for revision?

This is the work of language, belief, and logic. It's the level where systems are built. But it must come after context and embodiment. Because if we design our beliefs without reference to where we are or what we're made of, we will build brittle structures—maps with no terrain. This is where value is declared, and coherence is either established or fractured. Ask not just what you believe, but what that belief sustains.

Spiral Back — Trace the Changes

Once you've passed through all three, return to the environment. But see it now as changed.

Has my relationship to this space shifted?
Has my impact on others shifted?
Do I now perceive different options, constraints, or values?

The environment is never static. It responds to your changed perception and participation. As your consciousness evolves, so does your relational field. The spiral isn't a circle, it's an ascent. You are not returning to where you started. You are moving forward with more clarity, coherence, and capacity for service. This is where impact shows itself, in what becomes possible because of that change.

∾

THE SPIRAL AS LEXICON EMBODIED

To walk the spiral is to inhabit the lexicon:

> *Real is what moves you.*
> *Quality is how that movement feels.*
> *Value is what you begin to protect.*
> *Coherence is how you hold it together.*
> *Impact is what it leaves behind.*

None of these are fixed. All of them are alive. Practiced together, they don't just describe the world. They recompose your place within it.

FINAL INTEGRATION: THE SPIRAL LIVED

You are not asked to be perfect at all layers, all at once. You are invited to move through them with rhythm and care. This is what *Olamic Design* looks like in daily life. It's not a grand ideology. It's a design stance. It teaches us to slow down, trace our influence, name things with precision, align our actions with our beliefs, and place our beliefs in the service of life.

And when practiced over time, it builds something rare:

A person who can see clearly, act responsibly, and speak

with integrity, not because they know all the answers, but because they've learned how to listen across layers.

Not just "What do I want?"

But:

- What is the world asking for?
- What is this moment in relationship with?
- What becomes possible because I chose to participate?

This is the spiral lived. It is not a theory but a posture, not a tool but a way of being, not a sentence but a rhythm.

OLAM AND FOLAIGH

We've mentioned the name of this book series a few times: *Olam*. What we haven't done is talk about it directly.

The word is Hebrew. It means *the world*, as in *ha-olam hazeh, this world*. But in Hebrew, even the ordinary often conceals something older, stranger, more alive.

The root of *olam*, ʿayin-lamed-mem (עלם)—also gives rise to words that mean *to hide, to be veiled, to disappear*. A girl hidden from view is an *almah*. Something mysteriously lost is *ne'elam*. Even the Hebrew word for *eternity* (*l'olam*) gestures toward something unreachable; endless in time, yes, but also veiled from full grasp.

So while *olam* means *world*, it has always carried a trace of hiddenness within it, not just a place but a veil, not just the seen but the structure that conceals and reveals.

In Jewish mysticism, particularly the Kabbalistic systems that shaped medieval and early modern cosmology, *Olam* is not just this world, but one of many. The mystics spoke of four *Olamot* (worlds or realms), each nested within the other, filtering divine light into form:

- **Atzilut** (emanation)
- **Beriah** (creation)
- **Yetzirah** (formation)
- **Asiyah** (action)

These were not locations. They were filters of perception, veils of reality. To live in *Olam HaAsiyah*, the world of action, was to live inside the furthest reach of that light. Every *olam* was a layer between God and experience—a kind of metaphysical diffusion.

Olam HaNistar, "the hidden world," is not just a poetic phrase; it is a technical one. It is a statement that this world, the one we see, touch, and try to model, is inherently veiled. Its truths are partial. Its structures are folded. Its essence is hidden, not beyond, but *within*.

And that's the point.

In the language of Kabbalah, what's hidden is not somewhere else. It's right here. Hiddenness is not absence. It's embeddedness. The world is not lacking truth, it's made of it. We can't see it all at once.

That's the spiral this book has tried to trace: from instinct to story to system to structure, from the physical to the conceptual and back again. Every layer both reveals and conceals the one beneath it.

So when we call these books *Olam*, we aren't just naming the world. We're pointing to what the world conceals. And to the idea that every map we make is a partial view of something always larger, entangled, and hidden.

The visible is never the whole.

However, if we pay attention, live the spiral, speak with

care, and design with coherence, we may not remove the veil. But we might begin to trace its shape.

In that tracing, something sacred happens because **we become more capable of holding what we cannot fully see.**

My first encounter with the word *Olam* came during a conversation with a rabbi in New York in my late teens. I had grown up in a deeply Christian household, but in a town, Sharon, Massachusetts, where most of my neighbors, teachers, and friends were Jewish. I wasn't raised Jewish, but immersed in Jewish rituals, customs, and Kabbalistic thought from a young age. I was always drawn to its layered metaphors and living symbols.

In that conversation, I first heard the deeper resonance of *olam*; not just "the world," but *the hidden world*. The one we can't always see, but that's always there, just beneath the surface.

That idea didn't feel abstract. It felt true. It gave language to something I had always intuited: that the world is composed of partially visible systems, that much of what matters lies beneath perception, and that understanding is never about conquering mystery, but about turning toward it with care.

We live inside something vast and partially invisible, a reality too layered to fully grasp. That's what evolution does: it builds beings that can only perceive a fraction of the systems they're living in. This is true of our instincts. It's true of our beliefs. It's true of the impact we have.

But we've reached a point where this limitation has become more than background noise; it's dangerous. We've become too good at designing for what's directly in front of us, and not good enough at seeing what surrounds it. We can make something work while breaking everything that holds it together. This book is one attempt to interrupt that, to expand the field of what's worth noticing, and to remind us that design begins in perception.

More recently, I began learning Irish, a language rooted in myth, relationships, and landscape. I've always loved Irish for how it integrates story and environment.

Two words stood out to me:

Folaigh – the hidden.

Fios – knowledge.

But not knowledge as data. *Fios* is knowing that unfolds over time, through presence, attention, and uncovering what was always there. It's the flicker at the edge of recognition, the slow approach to understanding.

And *Fios* only makes sense because of *Folaigh*. Without the hidden, there is nothing to reveal. Without the veil, there is no shape to the seeing. *Olam* and *Folaigh* are related across languages. They name the same truth: that reality is not a flat surface, but a depth to be searched.

This book is part of that search. Not to unmask the world. But to learn how to move through it with humility.

Olam *is not a doctrine. It's a posture.*
A way of looking.
A way of staying close to the ground,
tethered to the animal we still are,
without giving up the mind we've built.
We don't need to know everything to live well.
We do need to know that something is always
    hidden.
Our job is to keep looking.

AN SNÁITHE I BHFÓLACH
THE HIDDEN THREAD

I wrote this modern myth to gather the ideas of this volume into a smaller vessel. I offer it to you now.

❧

There was once a girl in the western hills who had no craft.

She tried her hand at woodwork, but the tools splintered in her fingers.
She tried her voice in song, but the birds did not sing back.
She brewed tinctures, sewed cloth, studied the stars, walked with cattle—
But none claimed her.

Every elder said the same:
"You have no gift here. This is not your work."

So, she wandered, as the unwanted do.

Wherever she went, she gathered what was left behind by
trying:
A torn pattern, a broken pestle, an empty spindle, notes from a
song that didn't come.
Her pouch grew heavy, but she never put it down.

One dusk, by the ruins near a blackthorn grove, she met a
woman with one eye closed.
The woman asked nothing of her, only gesturing to sit.

So, she sat. Thin with walls, thick with witness.
And the old woman smiled like someone returning to breath.

Then, after a long while, the woman said,
"When Lugh came to Tara, the guards asked him:
What art have you, that you should be let in?"

The girl shook her head.

"He said: I am a smith. They answered, *We have a smith.*
I am a bard. *We have a bard.*
I am a healer. *We have a healer.*
And so it went, until he asked:
Do you have one who holds all these in one hand?

The girl breathed in.
The wind shifted.
The land knew her.
And *Fios* breathed out.

– Ian Terry

www.ingramcontent.com/pod-product-compliance
Lightning Source LLC
Chambersburg PA
CBHW051628120626

46551CB00014B/1992